Social and Emotional Development

The HighScope Preschool Curriculum

Social and Emotional Development

Ann S. Epstein, PhD

 HIGHSCOPE®

Published by

HighScope® Press

A division of the
HighScope Educational Research Foundation
600 North River Street
Ypsilanti, Michigan 48198-2898
734.485.2000, FAX 734.485.0704
Orders: 800.40.PRESS; Fax: 800.442.4FAX; www.highscope.org
E-mail: *press@highscope.org*

Editor: Jennifer Burd
Cover design: Phire Advertising and Design, LLC
Production: Judy Seling, Seling Design; Kazuko Sacks, Profit Makers LLC
Photography:
Gregory Fox — 1, 5, 6, 7, 13, 15, 17, 19, 21, 23, 24 (KDI 7, KDI 9), 25 (KDI 14, KDI 15), 28, 30, 33, 40, 41, 48, 51, 53, 57, 59, 61, 63, 71, 72, 75, 78, 83, 91, 92, 93, 95, 97, 98, 102, 106, 108, 111

Bob Foran — front and back covers, 24 (KDI 8, KDI 10, KDI 11), 25 (KDI 12, KDI 13), 27, 37, 38, 44, 47, 49, 58, 67, 68, 76, 77, 87, 88, 101, 105, 114, 116, 117 (upper and lower)

Library of Congress Cataloging-in-Publication Data
Epstein, Ann S.
  Social and emotional development / Ann S. Epstein, PhD.
      pages cm. -- (The HighScope preschool curriculum)
  Includes bibliographical references.
  ISBN 978-1-57379-652-1 (soft cover : alk. paper) 1. Child development.--Curricula. 2. Education, Preschool. I. Title.
  LB1115.E67 2012
  372.21--dc23
                                        2012004174

Printed in the United States of America
10 9 8 7 6 5

Contents

Acknowledgments

Many people contributed their knowledge and skills to the publication of *Social and Emotional Development*. I want to thank the early childhood and other staff members who collaborated on creating the key developmental indicators (KDIs) in this content area: Beth Marshall, Sue Gainsley, Shannon Lockhart, Polly Neill, Kay Rush, Julie Hoelscher, and Emily Thompson. Among this group of colleagues, those who devoted special attention to reviewing the manuscript for this book were Sue Gainsley and Emily Thompson. Mary Hohmann, whose expertise informs many other High-Scope curriculum books, also provided detailed feedback.

The developmental scaffolding charts in this volume — describing what children might do and say and how adults can support and gently extend their learning at different developmental levels — are invaluable contributions to the curriculum. I am grateful to Beth Marshall and Sue Gainsley for the extraordinary working relationship we forged in creating these charts. By bringing our unique experiences to this challenging process, we integrated knowledge about child development and effective classroom practices from the perspectives of research, teaching, training, and policy.

Thanks are also due to Nancy Brickman, who directed the editing and production of the book. I extend particular appreciation to Jennifer Burd, who edited the volume, and Katie Bruckner, who assisted with all aspects of the publication process. I also want to acknowledge the following individuals for contributing to the book's visual appeal and reader friendliness: photographers Bob Foran and Gregory Fox and graphic artists Judy Seling (book designer) and Kazuko Sacks (book production).

Finally, I extend sincerest thanks to all the teachers, trainers, children, and families whose participation in HighScope and other early childhood programs has contributed to the creation and authenticity of the HighScope Preschool Curriculum over the decades. I hope this book continues to support their social and emotional development for many years to come.

CHAPTER *1*

The Importance of Social and Emotional Development

Social and Emotional Development and Early Learning

Early childhood educators have long recognized the importance of supporting early social and emotional development. Today there is a growing awareness among other professionals (such as pediatricians), parents, policymakers, and the general public that social and emotional learning is equally, if not more important than, early academics, in determining school readiness. A good beginning in this content area affects not only whether young children succeed in school but also whether they will grow up to have rewarding personal and work lives, and contribute to society.

Children's early social and emotional relationships shape them for life. Interactions with family members set the stage for how they see themselves, whether they feel secure venturing out into the world, how they get along with others, and how they begin to understand moral behavior. Early childhood programs build on these home experiences and profoundly influence children's expanding relationships at school and in the community. They help children like Billy express his emotions, prepare Hannah and her peers to resolve social conflicts, ensure that children like Avalon know they matter, encourage Faith and Darla to play together, and support the spontaneity and emerging sense of humor displayed by friends such as Gabriel and José (see anecdotes at right).

Today's Special Challenges

Social-emotional development has always been a major concern of early childhood education. Today's practitioners face special challenges as they strive to support children confronted by

At greeting time, Billy says he is sad when his dad leaves. Then he sees his teacher Shannon and runs across the room to give her a big hug. "I'm happy you're back," he says.

At planning time, Hannah cries and says she wants to sit by Ellie, but two other children are already sitting by her. Chris, the teacher, acknowledges Hannah's feelings and asks the four children for their ideas on how to solve the problem. Hannah suggests the others can sit next to Ellie at planning time, and she will sit by Ellie at recall time. All four children agree to this idea. "You solved the problem," Chris tells them.

At work time in the house area, Avalon hands Sue (a former teacher who is filling in for the day) her name card. Avalon explains to Sue, "In case you have forgotten my name."

At outside time, Faith and Darla play in the sandbox making "goo pancakes." When their teacher comments that they are working together, Faith says, "Yeah, it's teamwork!"

At snacktime, Michelle (a teacher) asks Gabriel and José why they like to trick her. Gabriel says, "Because we are kids" and José adds, "And it's funny."

changing family dynamics, economic uncertainty, unsafe neighborhoods, the tragedies of war, and the devastation of natural disasters. Children are also subjected to academic pressures at ever younger ages. In addition to learning social norms at home and school, young children in the 21st century are exposed to growing influences from the media and technology, where they encounter evolving and often contradictory expectations for individual and interpersonal behavior. Children need inner resources to cope with these stresses.

The importance of early social as well as intellectual development is receiving renewed attention among educators, policymakers, parents, and the public as a whole. There is a growing backlash against a narrow focus on accountability in literacy and mathematics at the expense of social learning and problem-solving in the early childhood years. Landmark publications, such as *Eager to Learn* (National Research Council, 2001) and *From Neurons to Neighborhoods* (National Research Council and Institute of Medicine, 2000) summarize research showing that social and emotional learning is as much a part of a young child's school readiness as academic knowledge and skills.

W. Steven Barnett, Director of the National Institute for Early Education Research (NIEER), states that "one misconception about preschool education is that it's mostly about giving children an early start on the academic skills they'll need later. Maybe it's because early reading and math skills are more easily assessed or because parents and those who market to them often emphasize the academic side of children's early learning. Whatever the case, we run the risk of shortchanging the role preschool education plays in the broader cognitive, social, and emotional development of young children" (NIEER, 2007b, p. 2).

> "It is not easy to be a child in an early childhood program. Imagine experiencing it for the first time. You come into a strange building full of other children and adults who are strangers, full of enticing toys that are not your own....There are many things to learn about — but in order to learn you have to wade in and try things. Learning is hard work, and it involves taking risks...of being laughed at, of being wrong, of being ignored or rejected. Yet this desire for mastery is what leads to social and intellectual competence. It is almost impossible for children to have the courage to start on this journey without a foundation of emotional security."
>
> — Hyson (2004, p. 49)

What the Research Says

Jack Shonkoff, Director of the Center on the Developing Child at Harvard University, echoes this concern: "Emotional well-being and social competence provide a strong foundation for emerging cognitive abilities. Together they are the 'bricks and mortar' of the foundation of human development. The brain is a highly integrated organ. Social development and regulation of behavior are as much a part of development as cognitive learning. Preschool teachers should know as much about social and emotional development as teaching literacy. We [in the early childhood community] haven't done a good job of developing that" (NIEER, 2007a, p. 5).

Accompanying the general spotlight on social-emotional development is a specific focus on the many benefits of play. A report by the American Academy of Pediatrics (2006) received wide media coverage when it pleaded for the restoration of play to develop social-emotional skills such as building resilience, managing stress, and forming relationships with adults and peers, within and outside the family. The report advised, "As parents choose child care and early education programs for their children, pediatricians can reinforce the importance of choosing settings that offer more than 'academic preparedness.' They should be guided to also pay attention to the social and emotional development needs of the children" (p. 18).

More than a decade ago, psychologists Judy Dunn (1998) and Carolyn Saarni (1999) summarized a growing body of research that contradicted many traditional beliefs about early social and emotional development, particularly the notion that young children are egocentric. Toddlers and preschoolers are in fact very interested in how the feelings and beliefs of others compare to their own. Children between the ages of three and five develop an increasingly complex "theory of mind" to explain people's behavior with respect to their internal states. They progress from seeing intentions, desires, and feelings as motivators to understanding that thoughts and beliefs also guide behavior (Wellman, 2002). Older preschool children make generalizations based on personality. They recognize that people have enduring traits that affect their thoughts, feelings, and behavior (Giles & Heymann, 2005a & b). At this age, they can also identify a broader range of emotions, and can explain their causes and consequences ("You're mad because it keeps falling down!").

The Impact of Early Social and Emotional Experiences

Early social and emotional experiences can shape the rest of a child's life. While a child's first and primary relationships are at home, high-quality programs can support and supplement these family foundations. Interpersonal experiences are important in their own right as children learn to interact with adults and peers. These exchanges also provide a context to gain knowledge and skills in other areas. If the experience is positive, children become engaged and motivated learners. If the atmosphere is harsh or punitive, they may reject school and other sources of learning. For these reasons, young

---

Milestones in Social and Emotional Development

Infants
- Learn to regulate behaviors (e.g., crying, moving, focusing)
- Create bonds with primary caregivers and form a sense of trust from nurturing attachments

Toddlers
- Identify and gain control of their feelings
- Test their skills and begin to see themselves as capable
- Increasingly differentiate themselves from others and venture into the world of social interaction

Preschoolers
- Develop understanding of their own and others' feelings
- See themselves as doers, based on their ability to achieve self-initiated goals
- Widen their social network, developing preferences and forming friendships, and associating with new communities at home and school

— Epstein (2009, p. 13)

Children's interpersonal experiences help them gain knowledge and skills in other areas.

children depend on warm and nurturing environments to get a good start on formal education and lifelong learning.

Social-emotional development begins at birth and continues into adulthood. Depending on the security of their attachments with parents and other caregivers, children learn from their earliest experiences to view the world as a welcoming and exciting place or a trap to be approached with caution, a vacuum that is empty of love and stimulation, even a danger zone fraught with peril. A safe environment invites exploration while an untrustworthy one may lead to confusion, anger, or hopelessness. The way children are treated affects how they see and feel about themselves.

A child's early self-image, in turn, determines how he or she feels about the world, including how the child approaches learning and human relationships throughout the school years and

indeed, throughout life. Children's inner emotional well-being affects their outward-directed social selves. Psychologist Susanne Denham (2006) says that preschoolers who are more socially and emotionally perceptive are more successful in their relationships with age-mates and adults, which affects school readiness since early learning is so socially based. In other words, say Lilian Katz and Diane McClellan, "socially competent young children are those who engage in satisfying interactions and activities with adults and peers and through such interactions further improve their own competence" (1997, p. 1).

At work time in the block area, Leon dresses in a firefighter coat and hat. He says there's a fire and points to the toy area. When the teacher asks how he can stop the fire, Leon says he needs a hose. He pulls out a tape measure and says, "I have to open it til a big number shows because the hose has to be really long." He directs the hose at the fire and makes "swishing" noises. "There," he says, looking satisfied, "Now it's out and we can go back to the firehouse."

Social-emotional growth in the early years thus affects, and is affected by, virtually every other aspect of children's development. Infants are born with innate temperaments and individual dispositions that affect how they approach and deal with interpersonal experiences (Chess & Alexander, 1996). (See "Aspects of Temperament.") Preschoolers' expanding use of language and ability to form mental images allows them to better understand their own motivations and express their wishes to others, for example, when a child says, "I'm happy. My daddy's coming home today!" They also begin to recognize and name the emotions they see in others: "Betty is happy. I'll play with her." "Sammy's crying. He's sad because he wants his mom." This emerging ability to identify their own and others' needs and moods — that is, to better understand themselves and the perspective of others — helps young children decide when and how to approach others, with increasing success.

Aspects of Temperament

Although researchers differ on the number and nature of separate domains of temperament, most agree that any listing should include the following four dimensions (Rothbart and Bates, 1998):

- **Emotionality** is the degree to which the child's predominant affect is positive and happy or negative and distressed.

- **Inhibition** is the degree to which the child approaches and adapts to new situations or people with openness, trust, and curiosity or with avoidance, discomfort, or fear.

- **Activity** is the degree to which the child's characteristic level of motion is high and energetic or low and lethargic.

- **Sociability** is the degree to which the child responds to and initiates interactions with people or ignores and turns away from others.

Temperament plays a major role in early development (Teglasi & Epstein, 1998). It affects how adults react to the child and how the child chooses and interprets experiences. It is important to recognize that temperament acts in a continuous feedback loop. Temperamental differences determine both how the child deals with the world and how the world responds to the child.

Although temperament is based on genetics and biology, this does not mean quality of care is unimportant. On the contrary, says psychologist Ross Thompson (2009), "Children's interactions with parents, child care providers, and other people create an environment of relationships in which brain development unfolds and temperamental individuality is expressed" (p. 36). Adults need to be sensitive and responsive, respect emerging abilities, talk about emotions and how to manage them, and be flexible in adapting the environment to children's ever-changing needs.

The Developing Capacity for Relationships

The preschool child's developing capacity for relationships is also affected by the following three characteristics: a desire for friendship, a struggle to resolve the competition between "me" and "we," and growing social competence. These are each described here.

Desire for friendship

Children are social beings. Beginning in late toddlerhood and continuing throughout the preschool years, they expand their desire for relationships with adults to include associations with other children. In particular, they appear to seek friends who share their interests and approach activities with the same spirit of investigation. The basis of children's friendships is thus similar to that of adults.

At greeting time, Tasha sits on the couch and looks at a book with Joseph. When she goes to the table for small-group time, Tasha says, "I wanna sit next to Joseph."

❖

At small-group time, Marissa and Lee use the blocks and the dollhouse figures together. Their figures talk to each other, and they build structures for them.

Preschoolers do not always know how to create friendships. They may stand uncertainly on the sidelines or attempt to force their way into a group. Even children who are friends often fight over toys, ideas, or who gets to be the leader. But because the desire to connect with others is strong, young children are eager to learn the strategies that allow such connections to develop.

Children are social beings. Beginning in late toddlerhood, children's desire for relationships expands to include associations with other children.

"Me" versus "we"

Sometimes a child's need to do or get something conflicts with the desire for friendship. For example, a child may want to play firefighters with a friend but at the same time want to hold the hose the friend is carrying. The urge to be independent (the "me") does not always mesh with the longing to be part of the group (the "we"). Preschoolers are increasingly aware of the tensions that arise when these desires meet head on.

At work time in the block area, both Sklar and Lily want Carrie to be their dog. The teacher asks how they can solve the problem. Sklar says, "I can be a dog too, and Lily can be the owner for both dogs." Lily agrees to this idea and cuts long pieces of string for Sklar and Carrie to hold on to as leashes.

Teachers play a critical role in creating a supportive emotional climate in which children's conflicting desires are seen as normal, and problem solving can proceed in a nonjudgmental way. To become a participating group member, children must be able to give up some individuality for the greater good. Professors Richard Jantz and Carol Seefeldt (1999) see this transition from the "me" of toddlerhood to the "us" or "we" of preschool as the beginning of civic competence, or the ability to participate as a responsible citizen in society, which continues to develop into the elementary and adolescent years.

Social competence

Preschoolers gradually begin to sort out the conflicts described, such as what to do when their intentions clash with those of others or how to balance independence against a desire to join the group. As young children experience and understand the consequences of their actions, they can better choose between positive and negative social interactions. Using language to understand others and express themselves gives them a powerful tool to resolve conflicts in nonaggressive ways. And while they still focus on their own needs, young children are also increasingly aware of, and sensitive to, the needs and feelings of others. In fact, they are capable of empathy (discussed in chapter 6) much earlier than social scientists have long thought.

At work time in the block area, Natalie steps on Victor's train. She looks at his face and tells her teacher, "He's angry." With the teacher's help, Natalie fixes the train, and Victor says, "Now I'm happy." Natalie responds, "I like your smile!"

About This Book

In the HighScope Preschool Curriculum, the content of children's learning is organized into eight areas: A. Approaches to Learning; B. Social and Emotional Development; C. Physical Development and Health; D. Language, Literacy, and Communication; E. Mathematics; F. Creative Arts; G. Science and Technology; and H. Social Studies. Within each content area, HighScope identifies **key developmental indicators (KDIs)** that are the building blocks of young children's thinking and reasoning.

The term *key developmental indicators* encapsulates HighScope's approach to early education. The word *key* refers to the fact that these are the meaningful ideas children should learn and experience. The second part of the term — *developmental* — conveys the idea that learning is gradual and cumulative. Learning follows a sequence, generally moving from simple to more complex knowledge and skills. Finally, we chose the term *indicators* to emphasize that educators need evidence that children are developing the knowledge, skills, and understanding considered important for school and life readiness. To plan appropriately for students and to evaluate program effectiveness, we need observable indicators of our impact on children.

This book is designed to help you as you guide and support young children's learning in the Social and Emotional Development content area in the HighScope Curriculum. This chapter provided insights from research literature on children's developing awareness of feelings, capacity for relationships, and social competence. Chapter 2 describes general teaching strategies for Social and Emotional Development and provides an overview of the KDIs for this content area.

Chapters 3–11, respectively, provide specific teaching strategies for each of the nine KDIs in Social and Emotional Development:

7. **Self-identity:** Children have a positive self-identity.

8. **Sense of competence:** Children feel they are competent.

9. **Emotions:** Children recognize, label, and regulate their feelings.

10. **Empathy:** Children demonstrate empathy toward others.

11. **Community:** Children participate in the community of the classroom.

12. **Building relationships:** Children build relationships with other children and adults.

13. **Cooperative play:** Children engage in cooperative play.

14. **Moral development:** Children develop an internal sense of right and wrong.

15. **Conflict resolution:** Children resolve social conflicts.

At the end of each of these chapters is a chart showing ideas for scaffolding learning for that KDI. The chart will help you recognize the specific abilities that are developing at earlier, middle, and later stages of development and gives corresponding teaching strategies that adults can use to support and gently extend children's learning at each stage.

HighScope Preschool Curriculum Content
Key Developmental Indicators

A. Approaches to Learning

1. **Initiative:** Children demonstrate initiative as they explore their world.

2. **Planning:** Children make plans and follow through on their intentions.

3. **Engagement:** Children focus on activities that interest them.

4. **Problem solving:** Children solve problems encountered in play.

5. **Use of resources:** Children gather information and formulate ideas about their world.

6. **Reflection:** Children reflect on their experiences.

B. Social and Emotional Development

7. **Self-identity:** Children have a positive self-identity.

8. **Sense of competence:** Children feel they are competent.

9. **Emotions:** Children recognize, label, and regulate their feelings.

10. **Empathy:** Children demonstrate empathy toward others.

11. **Community:** Children participate in the community of the classroom.

12. **Building relationships:** Children build relationships with other children and adults.

13. **Cooperative play:** Children engage in cooperative play.

14. **Moral development:** Children develop an internal sense of right and wrong.

15. **Conflict resolution:** Children resolve social conflicts.

C. Physical Development and Health

16. **Gross-motor skills:** Children demonstrate strength, flexibility, balance, and timing in using their large muscles.

17. **Fine-motor skills:** Children demonstrate dexterity and hand-eye coordination in using their small muscles.

18. **Body awareness:** Children know about their bodies and how to navigate them in space.

19. **Personal care:** Children carry out personal care routines on their own.

20. **Healthy behavior:** Children engage in healthy practices.

D. Language, Literacy, and Communication[1]

21. **Comprehension:** Children understand language.

22. **Speaking:** Children express themselves using language.

23. **Vocabulary:** Children understand and use a variety of words and phrases.

24. **Phonological awareness:** Children identify distinct sounds in spoken language.

25. **Alphabetic knowledge:** Children identify letter names and their sounds.

26. **Reading:** Children read for pleasure and information.

27. **Concepts about print:** Children demonstrate knowledge about environmental print.

28. **Book knowledge:** Children demonstrate knowledge about books.

29. **Writing:** Children write for many different purposes.

30. **English language learning:** (If applicable) Children use English and their home language(s) (including sign language).

---

[1]Language, Literacy, and Communication KDIs 21–29 may be used for the child's home language(s) as well as English. KDI 30 refers specifically to English language learning.

E. Mathematics

31. **Number words and symbols**: Children recognize and use number words and symbols.

32. **Counting**: Children count things.

33. **Part-whole relationships**: Children combine and separate quantities of objects.

34. **Shapes**: Children identify, name, and describe shapes.

35. **Spatial awareness**: Children recognize spatial relationships among people and objects.

36. **Measuring**: Children measure to describe, compare, and order things.

37. **Unit**: Children understand and use the concept of unit.

38. **Patterns**: Children identify, describe, copy, complete, and create patterns.

39. **Data analysis**: Children use information about quantity to draw conclusions, make decisions, and solve problems.

F. Creative Arts

40. **Art**: Children express and represent what they observe, think, imagine, and feel through two- and three-dimensional art.

41. **Music**: Children express and represent what they observe, think, imagine, and feel through music.

42. **Movement**: Children express and represent what they observe, think, imagine, and feel through movement.

43. **Pretend play**: Children express and represent what they observe, think, imagine, and feel through pretend play.

44. **Appreciating the arts**: Children appreciate the creative arts.

G. Science and Technology

45. **Observing**: Children observe the materials and processes in their environment.

46. **Classifying**: Children classify materials, actions, people, and events.

47. **Experimenting**: Children experiment to test their ideas.

48. **Predicting**: Children predict what they expect will happen.

49. **Drawing conclusions**: Children draw conclusions based on their experiences and observations.

50. **Communicating ideas**: Children communicate their ideas about the characteristics of things and how they work.

51. **Natural and physical world**: Children gather knowledge about the natural and physical world.

52. **Tools and technology**: Children explore and use tools and technology.

H. Social Studies

53. **Diversity**: Children understand that people have diverse characteristics, interests, and abilities.

54. **Community roles**: Children recognize that people have different roles and functions in the community.

55. **Decision making**: Children participate in making classroom decisions.

56. **Geography**: Children recognize and interpret features and locations in their environment.

57. **History**: Children understand past, present, and future.

58. **Ecology**: Children understand the importance of taking care of their environment.

General Teaching Strategies for Social and Emotional Development

General Teaching Strategies

A warm and predictable environment that is responsive to children's needs builds trusting and healthy relationships. This supportive climate strengthens the child's ability to approach the world with confidence and master new challenges. In the preschool years, children grow in their capacity to participate in the world beyond the family. They learn to respect themselves and to serve as a resource to others, to express their thoughts and feelings and negotiate for what they want, to lead and to follow, and to be actively involved in the many complex aspects of human relationships. The following teaching practices can help to set the stage for these developments.

Create a supportive environment

Children learn and thrive when they feel emotionally secure and are socially connected to adults who provide nurturance and positive opportunities for learning. For both emotional and social learning, then, the central role of adults is to create a warm and caring program environment.

Adults establish a safe and secure setting by understanding the challenges children face when they find themselves among strangers, in an unfamiliar place, and with new expectations for behavior. Even if the values of home and school are congruent, the group nature of the classroom creates a different set of personal and social norms. By creating a supportive climate, teachers can help preschoolers discover themselves and begin to establish positive relationships with others. To the extent that children can develop these abilities on their own — with adults providing support as needed — their feelings of social and emotional confidence will be enhanced.

At work time in the house area, Mackenzye tries to remove the tab from a diaper. She tries two ways until it finally pulls off. She tries putting another diaper on her doll and throws it down in frustration. Her teacher asks if she wants help. When Mackenzye says yes, the teacher says Ben knows how to do it if she'd like to ask him. Mackenzye says to Ben, "Can you help me put the diaper on my baby?" "Go like this," Ben says, sliding his finger under the tab to pry it free. "Now you try," he says, and Mackenzye successfully loosens and attaches the other side.

For more information on establishing a supportive climate, see chapter 2 in *The HighScope Preschool Curriculum* (Epstein & Hohmann, 2012).

Help children make the transition from home to school

When young children enter the early childhood classroom, their primary attachments are still centered at home or with significant others who care for them throughout the day. Teachers, working with family members, play a crucial role in helping children make a successful transition from these familiar people and places to the school setting.

To help young children transition from home to school, support them through separations until they are confident they can handle them on their own. Acknowledge and accept their feelings about being apart from family members and their worries about whether a parent will return later to take them home. Encourage family members to stay as long as they can while a child settles in, and allow children to enter activities at their own pace.

Christina arrives at preschool with tears in her eyes. Clutching a doll, she hugs her mother's knees without looking at her teacher, who kneels

At greeting time, teachers and parents join in an activity that helps children transition from home to school.

on the floor to greet her. When her mother leaves, Christina's teacher gives her a hug, and hand-in-hand they walk to the book area to find Christina's favorite book. After a month, when Christina has become accustomed to the new routine, she gets to the school door before her mother and hurries inside to greet her friends and choose a book. "Bye, Mom," she says as she waves from the greeting circle.

Remember that sometimes even children who separate easily have trouble saying good-bye now and then. For example, if a parent is reading to them, they may simply want this plea-surable activity to go on for a while longer. Also, be alert to signs of separation anxiety that may emerge other than at dropoff time. For example, pretending to go to the doctor may remind a child of feeling alone during a scary medical procedure. Even putting on coats at the end of

the day may awaken a child's worries about a parent's return, especially if there have been past incidents of a parent being late or forgetting whose turn it was to pick up the child.

Family stresses, such as the birth of a sibling or a parent's illness, or even a positive event such as a grandparent's visit, can also cause children to worry about being lost in the con-fusion or excitement. Reassure them that they are valued members of their families and the classroom, and that who they are and their well-being are important to all the adults who care for them. Children may benefit from having a family picture they can carry around with them, or a class book with photographs from every child's family that they can curl up with in the book area for reassurance.

At work time, Jacob's teacher kneels beside him as Jacob (whose mother is incarcerated) talks about the mother and baby hamsters in the cage. "She's loving them," he says about the mother. He puts his head on the teacher's shoulder and she holds him and strokes his back. "It looks like you are feeling sad," she says, and Jacob presses up against her and nods.

Arrange and equip the classroom for social interactions

As described in chapter 6 of *The HighScope Preschool Curriculum* (Epstein & Hohmann, 2012), designing the classroom space and providing appropriate materials are fundamental to promoting active learning in general. These features are also essential elements in specifically supporting early affective development. Research shows that how the classroom is arranged affects the interactions that take place within it (Cummings, 2000). For example, an observational study by researchers Mary Louise Hemmeter and Michelle Ostrosky (2003) found that children interacted at higher levels when they worked in classroom areas that accommodated several children rather than one or two, and played with toys conducive to multiple users rather solitary play. Children in these settings engaged in complex play, communicated more with one another as well as adults, and had fewer disagreements than children in settings with limited space and play-alone toys.

At work time in the block area, Delia and Yvonne pretend to be kitties. They build beds out of long blocks and line them with blankets from the house area. Using small square blocks as bowls, they lap up "milk" and make mewing noises. After a while, Delia begins to bark softly. She says to Yvonne, "You can be a nice cat and I can be a nice dog." She calls a wooden dowel her "bone" and gives Yvonne a counting bear to use as the cat's "mouse toy." They continue to play animals until cleanup time.

Accommodating different-sized groups.
To promote social interactions and a sense of community, arrange the classroom so different size groups can gather and move freely between areas. Include open areas where large groups can assemble and small enclosed areas with comfortable furniture for intimate interactions. When spaces are tight, children are forced to play on their own or in limited groups. Restricting the number who can work in an area creates competition and contradicts the idea of the classroom as a community. In HighScope settings, no area is limited. If an area is very popular, teachers find a way to increase its size by rearranging furniture or opening access to the area next to it.

For example, if the computer is in a corner with one chair, then working there becomes an activity for a single child. If, on the other hand, the computer is in an open space with two or more chairs, working there can be a shared activity with children using the keyboard, contributing ideas, and talking about what is on the screen. In fact, observational research shows preschoolers prefer to use the computer communally rather than individually (Clements, 1999).

Conversely, when the classroom is a big and undivided space, children may feel overwhelmed by how impersonal (and noisy and bustling) the setting is. While some children thrive in a beehive of activity, others experience difficulty finding their "place" in this undifferentiated community. Even children who do well in large groups may sometimes want to curl up alone with the teacher to look at a book, or work quietly at a small table to make a collage with a friend. A variety of intimate and open spaces allows children with different temperaments or fluctuating needs to find a setting that is right for them. Teachers can also interact with children one-on-one or in small and large groups, again depending on what they sense is called for at any given moment.

Limiting clutter. Another consideration in arranging the room to promote emotional and social development is to limit the amount of clutter. This lessens the chance that children will be overwhelmed, especially at the beginning of the year when everything is new and exciting to them. Uncluttered spaces also make it possible for children to congregate and act out their play ideas without feeling crowded or worrying about bumping into or breaking things. They can spread their play into adjoining areas and more easily carry materials from one area to another.

At work time in the block area, when other children cannot get to the block shelf because so many blocks are on the floor, Gina clears a path for them. Dee and Chloe carry small blocks back to the house area, where they sit on the couch and feed their dolls wooden "Popsicles." Together with Gina, four other children continue to build a hockey rink on one side of the path. Justin takes a long block he calls a "police flashlight" and sits inside the chairs-and-blanket tent he's built with Rona, looking at photographs of his family's camping trip.

At work time in the house area, Aubrey plays with two other girls. She takes dishes out of the cupboard and says, "Okay, kids. We have a big day today. We're moving." As they begin to stack dishes, Aubrey puts her hands on her hips and says, "What on earth can we pack these in?" She goes to the block area, empties a plastic crate, and tells the boys playing there she needs it for moving. Two of them volunteer to be the movers. "Come on," says Aubrey, "we gotta finish and get there before it gets dark!"

Choosing materials. The kinds of materials the classroom is stocked with can also have a big impact on children's social interactions.

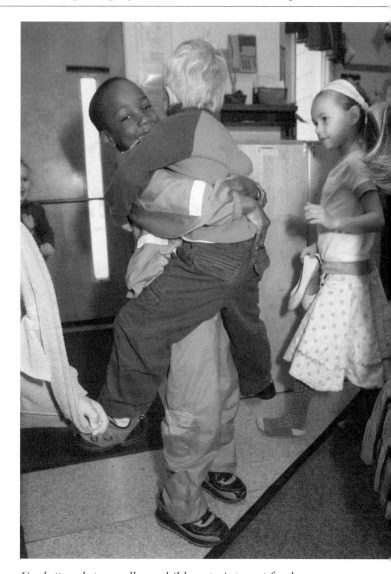

Uncluttered space allows children to interact freely.

Choose materials that inspire group role play (such as dress-up clothes) and outdoor equipment (such as long, multiwheeled vehicles) that requires two or more children to operate. Large and heavy objects, such as oversized blocks or water-filled pails, also encourage children to work in teams to achieve their goals. Whenever possible, provide enough of the same type of materials so children can use them side by side and together. If they are preoccupied with having access to materials, they are less likely to think about how to use them together.

This strategy is supported by the HighScope Training for Quality study (Epstein, 1993), which found that when children had access to plentiful and diverse materials they could retrieve and put away on their own, they played more productively and had fewer social conflicts. In sum, by simultaneously supporting children's self-sufficiency (enabling them to manage on their own without frustration or competition for resources) and also enabling spontaneous interactions (through areas and materials that encourage collaboration), adults can create a physical space conducive to children's early social and emotional development.

At work time in the woodworking area, Shannon (a teacher) tells Ashley that she needs to wear goggles. Jerzy stops what he is doing, goes to the shelf, gets a pair of goggles and hands them to Ashley. After she puts them on, she asks him, "Do you want me to hold your board so you can pound in the (golf) tees?" Ashley and Jerzy take turns helping one another create designs in the foam boards with colored golf tees.

Implement predictable schedules and routines to create a secure community

A consistent daily routine is an important feature of every active learning classroom. Preschoolers learn important concepts about time, sequencing, and organization. Predictability also promotes social and emotional development by helping children feel secure and in control of the day's events. Further, a balanced schedule provides opportunities for working individually and in different social configurations, including pairs, small groups, and large groups.

At planning time, Sienna says she wants to play with Nadine. When the teacher asks what they will do, Sienna turns to her friend and asks,

"What do you want to do?" Nadine replies, "Play hospital. I'll be a shot doctor and you be a medicine doctor." They go to the house area where they put dolls and a medical kit on the table. They "cook" special medicine on the stove, and use colored markers from the art area as syringes to give their sick babies "shots." At one point, Sienna looks at the clock, holds up the fingers on one hand, and tells Nadine, "We still have five minutes." Sienna and Nadine continue to play hospital until work time ends.

Because it is shared, the daily routine creates a social community through "time" in the same way that the room arrangement creates one through "space." When everyone is engaged in the same type of activity at the same time each day, it creates a feeling of commonality and togetherness. Note that participating in the same *type* of activity does not mean everyone does the same thing. Children can be equally engaged but work with materials and ideas in different ways. What all the children share at such periods is a commonality of purpose — learning through experience — that is taking place at the same time and within the same routine structure. Choice promotes their sense of autonomy, which in turn makes their voluntary membership in the group authentic.

Another aspect of the daily routine that can promote social interaction and a sense of community is for each activity to proceed at an unhurried pace. That doesn't mean the schedule expands and contracts, only that each time slot is not crammed too full or fraught with expectations about what must get accomplished. A relaxed — yet consistent — schedule lets people enjoy one another's company instead of making them feel pressured to finish a task. Whether young children work together, or engage in conversation with adults and peers while carrying out parallel activities, freedom from time constraints helps them ease into the camaraderie of their social community.

A well-designed daily routine can also help to prevent challenging behaviors. Hemmeter and Ostrosky (2003) reported that young children were less disruptive and demonstrated more complex social interaction during longer play periods. Sustained engagement supported their emerging sense of competence and encouraged conversation and collaboration. These same characteristics have been observed during the extended work time of children enrolled in HighScope programs (Sylva, 1992). Hemmeter and Ostrosky also found that preschoolers were less anxious and more cooperative when there was flexibility about changing activities. In HighScope programs, children are encouraged to bring closure to whatever they are doing, and they also know they can continue working the next day on the things that interest them. Giving children a signal before ending an activity helps them prepare for the change.

At small-group time, Bethany puts a row of tiny clay balls on a rectangle of cardboard. When she finishes the first row, she begins a second row underneath it. At the end of group time, she is halfway through the third row. As the other children clean up and move to the rug for large-group time, Bethany completes the row she is working on. Her teacher helps her wrap the remaining clay balls in plastic and carry the cardboard to a shelf. Bethany puts a "work-in-progress sign" next to it. "I'm gonna make a plan to finish it tomorrow," she tells her teacher.

Foster specific skills through modeling, coaching, and providing opportunities for practice

Young children develop social and emotional skills through direct experience rather than direct instruction. Katz and McClellan (1997)

caution in *Fostering Children's Social Competence: The Teacher's Role* that "lessons, lectures, magic circles, workbook exercises, or suggestive and sometimes exhortatory approaches [do not work, especially] when they are attempted with the class as a whole" (p. 20). However, "individualized guidance" can work because it maximizes a child's participation in constructing new knowledge and allows the teacher to be warm and supportive during the interaction. Three techniques in particular work well with preschoolers:

Modeling. "Teaching by example, or modeling, is the most powerful technique that educators employ, intentionally or otherwise" (Elias et al., 1997, p. 56). Children learn appropriate behavior when they see teachers being empathic, problem-solving social conflicts, taking emotional risks, and admitting mistakes. Modeling enables children to pick up knowledge

A predictable daily routine promotes sustained engagement, collaboration, and conversation.

and skills through their own observations, but social learning is enhanced when teachers occasionally make explicit what they are doing. For example, teachers might point out how they are listening to each child during a group activity or class discussion. Raising children's awareness that they are engaged in "social learning" also identifies it as a domain of instruction on a par with reading or mathematics, rather than a diversion from "real" education in the classroom.

Mental health professors Lise Fox and Rochelle Harper Lentini (2006) say modeling is most effective when it is embedded in the meaningful activities that happen during a child's day. For example, while playing with a group of children, the teacher might comment, "It looks like you need another big block. I'll share one of mine with you." Puppets, dolls, and stuffed animals are also useful in modeling social skills. Play figures can act out a problem, talk about the feelings it evokes, and dialogue with teachers and students about possible solutions.

Coaching. Coaching is breaking a behavior into its components, explaining how to perform and sequence the parts, creating opportunities for practice (see the following section), and giving feedback on the child's efforts. Coaching social skills — also called "play tutoring" — works the same way as providing instruction in other domains such as literacy or physical movement.

Coaching may be especially helpful with children who do not seem to be accepted by their peers and whose resulting anger only increases their rejection and ostracism. For example, a teacher might coach a child who is having trouble entering into an ongoing play group on how to initially observe from the sidelines, offer to help with some task that will further the group's play (fetching blocks for a building), accept a role assigned by the leader rather than forcibly entering or trying to take over the direction of play, or notice the cues that

indicate the group is now open to the child's entry (the others move over to make room for the new player).

At planning time, Joey says, "I'm going to the computer." When told both computers are in use, he frowns and tenses his body. Then he remembers what his teacher suggested the day before. "Maybe I can watch them," he says, "and then I can play." He pulls up an extra chair and watches the other children work with a drawing program. "You could put a dog there," Joey suggests, and one of them does while moving over to make room for Joey at the keyboard. All three children share ideas, try them out, and comment on the results. At recall time, Joey announces proudly, "Me and Ali and Kevin all played on the computer."

Fox and Lentini (2006) suggest using prompts as a follow-up to coaching. A teacher can give a verbal, visual, or physical cue to help children remember to use a skill in which they have been coached. For example, as a child moves toward a group, the teacher might coach him or her to ask to play. Giving encouragement afterward also helps children know they've mastered a skill. For example, you might describe what the child did and the reaction you saw, such as, "You asked Manny for a turn, and then I saw the two of you playing together in the block area."

Providing opportunities for practice. As in any other domain, repetition and practice are also vital to learning social behavior. For some children, moving from acquiring to generalizing a skill occurs easily and with little adult intervention. Other children need more systematic help to practice what they are learning and apply it to different scenarios. In these cases, teachers can look out for and encourage children to use their new-found skills in comparable situations.

Through modeling, teachers can show children how to interact with one another.

For example, Fox and Lentini (2006, p. 41) describe a preschooler who used the steps of problem-solving in the classroom but did not apply them on the playground or on field trips. During a visit to a hands-on museum, the teacher knelt next to him as he approached an activity station where children were playing with magnets. To help prevent a potential conflict, she acknowledged his desire to play with the other children and asked what he could do to join them. She quietly went over the problem-solving steps with him and stayed nearby for support. When the child asked another child, "Can I play too?" he was offered a magnet and the two children built with magnets together. The teacher provided encouraging feedback by giving the child a wink and a smile.

Although social and emotional learning takes practice and generalization like other disciplines, it is also distinct because it entails not only the learning of new skills but also the "unlearning of habitual patterns of thought and behavior" (Elias et al., 1997, p. 55). Unlearning may be easier in preschool than later, when habits are ingrained. Nonetheless, norms in preschool and other settings can be incongruent. For example, listening to others may not be valued or practiced as much at home as in the classroom — all the more reason for classroom teachers to give young children repeated opportunities to integrate social skills into their everyday behavior until the skills become natural and routine. Once social skills become automatic, they are also more likely to be generalized from the early childhood setting into kindergarten and beyond.

Key Developmental Indicators

HighScope has nine **key developmental indicators (KDIs)** in Social and Emotional Development: 7. Self-identity, 8. Sense of competence, 9. Emotions, 10. Empathy, 11. Community, 12. Building relationships, 13. Cooperative play, 14. Moral development, and 15. Conflict resolution.

In social and emotional learning, perhaps more than any other content area of development, the components are highly interdependent. It is like a tree whose trunk grows from a newborn's undifferentiated self to a gathering awareness of emotional states and social relationships. Once the trunk reaches a certain height and thickness, limbs begin to form. Each limb corresponds to one of the KDIs. As the tree — the child — grows, each limb in turn sprouts branches and twigs. So, for example, in the limb for "emotions," children become aware that they have feelings and begin to label them, grow in their capacity to regulate their emotions, pay attention to the emotions of others, and consider how their own feelings are or are not like those of the people they interact with. In the limb for "building relationships," children build a primary relationship with an adult, relate to other adults, begin to interact with peers, and eventually form genuine friendships. Thus a child's social and emotional learning becomes increasingly differentiated. Like a tree, however, all branches lead back to and are dependent upon having a solid trunk.

Chapters 3–11 discuss early learning for each of the social and emotional KDIs and the specific teaching strategies adults can use to support their development. At the end of each chapter is a "scaffolding chart" with examples of what children might say and do at early, middle, and later stages of development and how adults can scaffold their learning through appropriate support and gentle extensions. These charts offer additional ideas on how you might carry out the strategies in the following chapters during play and other interactions with children.

Key Developmental Indicators in Social and Emotional Development

B. Social and Emotional Development

7. Self-identity: Children have a positive self-identity.

Description: Children are aware of the characteristics that make up their identity, such as gender, ethnicity, culture, and abilities. They perceive their uniqueness and develop a healthy self-image.

8. Sense of competence: Children feel they are competent.

Description: Children make discoveries and solve problems with an expectation of success. They believe they can acquire the knowledge or skills they need.

9. Emotions: Children recognize, label, and regulate their feelings.

Description: Children identify and name their emotions, and recognize that others have feelings that may be the same as or different from their own. They regulate the expression of their feelings.

10. Empathy: Children demonstrate empathy toward others.

Description: Children understand the feelings of others by drawing on their own experiences with the same emotions. They respond empathically by sharing the happiness of others and offering assistance when they see that others are emotionally upset or physically hurt.

11. Community: Children participate in the community of the classroom.

Description: Children act as members of the classroom community by participating in routines, cooperating with social expectations, and sharing responsibility for maintaining the classroom.

12. Building relationships: Children build relationships with other children and adults.

Description: Children relate to others in the classroom. They refer to teachers and peers by name. Children develop friendships, seek out others, and engage in give-and-take interactions.

13. Cooperative play: Children engage in cooperative play.

Description: Children involve adults and peers in their play. They engage in cooperative play with others by sharing materials, space, conversation, and ideas.

14. Moral development: Children develop an internal sense of right and wrong.

Description: Children develop ethical behavior. They understand that there are moral principles that do not vary by situation (e.g., people should not hit others).

15. Conflict resolution: Children resolve social conflicts.

Description: Children engage in conflict resolution, or social problem solving, to settle interpersonal differences. They identify the problem, offer and listen to others' ideas, and choose a solution that is agreeable to all.

Social and Emotional Development in Action

KDI 7. Self-identity

KDI 9. Emotions

KDI 10. Empathy

KDI 8. Sense of competence

KDI 11. Community

KDI 12. Building relationships

KDI 13. Cooperative play

KDI 14. Moral development

KDI 15. Conflict resolution

CHAPTER 3

KDI 7. Self-Identity

B. Social and Emotional Development
7. Self-identity: Children have a positive self-identity.

Description: Children are aware of the characteristics that make up their identity, such as gender, ethnicity, culture, and abilities. They perceive their uniqueness and develop a healthy self-image.

At snack time, Lindsay announces, "I went with my mommy to vote yesterday. She says girls can be a president when they grow up."

At the end of outside time, Mark's father comes to pick him up. "We're going to my daddy's new house," Mark says with a mix of excitement and apprehension. The next day, Mark's teacher asks about his father's apartment. "There's a swimming pool," he says and describes the new friend he made there. After a pause, Mark says he is lucky. When his teacher agrees, he adds, "I get to have two houses. My mommy's has a park and my daddy's has a pool."

At greeting time, Dolores runs up to her teacher and exclaims, "We went to the pow wow yesterday. I danced the bear dance with my grandpa!"

How Self-Identity Develops

Self-identity refers to how we see and feel about ourselves as people. Identity is who we are (girl or boy, brown- or blue-eyed), as opposed to what we can do (see KDI 8. Sense of competence). To develop social and emotional competence, children must feel good about themselves and believe they will be seen positively by others. Teachers, together with families and community members, play a vital role in the formation of children's earliest self-perceptions. By helping preschoolers discover who they are and by accepting them in all their diversity, early childhood educators can establish the fertile soil within which positive self-identity blooms.

The roots of self-identity

A sense of identity emerges as children become aware of their own characteristics, such as their gender, culture (which may include race, ethnicity, language, religion, place of origin), social class (as evidenced by possessions), family composition and birth order, physical traits (such as body build, hair texture, or skin color), and physical (dis)abilities (such as speed and dexterity or limitations in vision, hearing, or mobility). Whether children feel positively or negatively about themselves depends in large part on how these characteristics are valued by others, beginning with family members and later expanding to teachers and friends, and eventually to societal judgments as a whole.

The healthy development of one's individual identity depends on establishing trusting and secure relationships, especially early in life. Research shows that a sense of self first appears as infants realize that they and the people caring for them are not extensions of one another, but separate beings (Post, Hohmann, & Epstein, 2011). Identity formation continues into preschool and proceeds positively thereafter if and when children learn to respect their personal characteristics.

Identifying oneself and others

The young child's way of thinking can make for some interesting — and challenging — ideas about identity. For example, because preschoolers are concrete, they may focus on one aspect of gender identity and ignore another that seems to contradict it, saying, for example, that a boy baby with curls must be a girl. Their need to sort things can also make them somewhat rigid. For example, they might insist that only children who are "as tall as the door knob" are old enough to go to kindergarten. Identity formation thus involves not only understanding the categories that define people, but applying them with a balance of consistency and flexibility. This can be difficult for preschool children.

However, research shows that older preschoolers can increasingly look beyond appearance and behavior in their self-perceptions. For example, Herbert Marsh and his colleagues found that even four-year-olds have a dawning understanding of their psychological selves (Marsh, Ellis, & Craven, 2002), seeing themselves, for example, as ones who approach novelty with gusto or with caution. As they develop "theories of mind" about how "unobservable" mental properties such as thoughts operate, preschoolers incorporate social comparison information into their self-perceptions as

well (Pomerantz, Ruble, Frey, & Greulich, 1995), observing, for example, that "Me and Chris like to go on the bus with our grandpas."

The complex nature of developing an identity means that the process often extends well into adulthood. However, developmental psychologists have found that certain ideas about the self are already well-established by the preschool years (Ramsey, 2006). For example, it has long been established that *racial awareness* begins in toddlerhood and that children know their own race — including whether they are of mixed race — by preschool (Clark & Clark, 1947; Ramsey, 1991).

At small-group time, Kelly draws her self-portrait in oil pastels, looking at the color of her arm for comparison. She blends the skin color with shades of brown to make the face "more real." After she finishes, she holds up the paper and says, "Now it looks like me. I will take it home to show my mom."

Although preschoolers have no abstract concept of *social class,* they already perceive differences in wealth as shown by the number of possessions they and others have (Harrah & Friedman, 1990). There is little research on the effects of consumer culture on young children's self-identity, but preliminary studies show that even preschoolers may begin to classify themselves as "have nots" when surrounded by screen images of children who have more (Ramsey, 2006).

Likewise, young children have no notion of *culture,* yet they recognize and respond appropriately to differences in its practical manifestations, such as speech or dress (Orellana, 1994). For example, bilingual children know when to switch languages depending on the setting and/or the people with whom they are conversing. Furthermore, preschoolers often associate differences in language with differences in appearance, styles of clothing, or the places people live (Hirschfield & Gelman, 1997). They can't always explain the connection, but they sense it.

Anthony: I think I'm from Irish and something else.

Teacher: How do you know you're Irish?

Anthony: Because I have freckles like my mommy.

Teacher: What about the something else?

Anthony: *(Thinks a minute.)* Just from Irish. *(Pauses)* But not my daddy.

Gender identity and gender stereotypes are already well-established by preschool, and can affect children's behavior, career aspirations, peer interactions, and self-esteem (Bigler, 1997). Young children see gender as relatively stable, but do not always realize it is constant regardless of appearance or behavior. For example, a child may know she is a girl but say she wants to be a "daddy" when she grows up so she can cut the grass with a riding mower. The need for clear-cut categories can sometimes make preschoolers inflexible about such stereotypes.

Children try on different roles as they develop a sense of their identity.

However, as they begin to recognize things can belong to more than one category, children begin to accept broader notions of identity. Most important in achieving this flexibility is observing things that contradict their assumptions, for example, seeing or reading a book about a woman cutting the lawn.

Finally, research into preschoolers' beliefs about *disabilities* shows their ideas vary by the type of disability (Diamond & Innes, 2001). The more evident the disability — such as orthopedic and sensory limitations — the greater the children's awareness of difference on some dimension. Their explanations also reflect their concrete level of thinking. Preschoolers focus on the equipment in explaining a person's special needs ("He can't see because he wears special glasses"), the person's age or immaturity ("She hasn't learned how to walk yet"), or illness, injury, and trauma ("She had a really bad earache so now she can't hear"). Regardless of the nature of people's disabilities, however, preschoolers tend to see disabled persons as potential friends — much as they would any other child — and all children benefit from attending diverse and integrated classrooms. Nondisabled children tend to become more sensitive, while children with disabilities tend to develop a more accepting and less limiting sense of self. Children in both groups perceive their sameness to one another, more so than their differences.

In fact, this awareness and acceptance of similarities and differences lies at the heart of all children developing a positive self-identity as well as appreciating the diversity all around them. As they learn about themselves and their backgrounds, preschoolers come to see that they and others are made of many defining characteristics. This simply becomes, in their minds, what makes us who we are.

Teaching Strategies That Support Self-Identity

To help children establish and maintain a positive self-identity, adults can use the teaching strategies suggested here.

Focus on children throughout the day

Spend most of your time interacting with the children, rather than arranging materials, cleaning up, or conversing with other adults in the classroom. Your focused attention lets children know you value them as individuals, and are interested in what matters to them. Interact with children in calm, respectful tones. Never shout, shame, utter derogatory words, or use harsh language and actions in your dealings with any child. Finally, address your comments directly to children. Do not talk "about" children in front of them, as though they were not there.

When Carson's mother comes to pick him up, she asks his teacher Leona how her son's day has gone. Leona kneels beside Carson and says to him, "You and Jacob built a grain elevator during work time." Jacob eagerly describes to his mother and teacher how they used long blocks and lots of buckets. He is still talking about it as he and his mother head to the car.

Address diversity and differences positively

Preschoolers are curious about the differences they observe in people and are not shy about asking questions. Answer them in a straightforward manner and a conversational voice, the same way you would address their questions about the attributes of objects or events. Provide neutral labels to describe gender, skin color, family composition, religion, and other aspects of identity. Use common characteristics to sort children for transitions or games (e.g., "Everyone who has a brother, put on your coat for outside time"). Display photos or make "all about me" books that depict children and their families and discuss their varied characteristics. Draw self-portraits and family pictures at small-group time and encourage children to describe their drawings. Talking with children about differences in appearance and behavior can be both affirming and instructive as long as your tone is accepting and factual, not judgmental.

At greeting time, their preschool teacher comments to two girls, "You're both wearing flowered headbands in your hair today. Inaya's band is red and her hair is dark brown and curly. Aggie's headband is blue and her hair is blond and straight." The girls look in the mirror and smile at one another. At work time, they wrap scarves around their baby dolls.

❖

At small-group time, the children draw pictures of their families. Les says, "It's just me and my mom, so I only need a little paper." Magda takes two pieces of paper "because I have two families, one with my mom and one with my dad." Their teacher comments, "Each family is different. Some are small and some are big." Jeremy chimes in, "I live in two houses just like Magda." Susannah names the members of her family as she counts them off on her fingers.

Provide nonstereotyped materials, activities, and role models

Share books, stories, and songs in which people with different attributes and backgrounds feel good about themselves and establish positive relationships with others who are both the same and different from them. Provide materials and activities that defy traditional stereotypes, for example, picture books that depict women as construction workers, men doing housework, and senior citizens being active in jobs or other activities. Make sure dolls, play figures, picture books, and artwork represent a variety of cultural groups. Offer clothes and props for all children to role play different occupations, and encourage them to work with different types of equipment (carpentry tools, cooking utensils). Look for books and magazine photos that show elderly people and those with disabilities involved in a variety of activities that young and able-bodied people typically do. Talk about the accommodations they may need to make, but emphasize how they still perform and enjoy these activities.

At work time in the house area, Christian says, "I'm the maker. I make some pancakes and some food." He pretends to make and serve pancakes to his teacher.

❖

At work time in the construction area, Gayla uses a screwdriver to take apart an alarm clock. "These are the gears," she tells Milton, her teacher. "Show me how they work," he asks. Gayla makes circular motions in opposite directions with her forefingers. "They go around like this," she explains, "and catch each other. I help my uncle Joe (a jeweler) fix them."

❖

The children substitute words for the chant, "Five Little Monkeys Jumping on the Bed." Aaron suggests "elephants." When it is Wylie's turn, he says, "five grandmas jumping on the bed." "My granny has a trampoline," says Chloe as she begins to bounce up and down.

Both boys and girls enjoy playing "house" as they explore their identities.

Encourage family members to become involved in the program

The first source of identity is the family. Preschoolers introduce the members of their family to others as a way of proclaiming who they are. Inviting family members to be part of the program helps to affirm and validate a child's emerging self-concept. Since many family members are often regularly involved with caregiving, don't limit involvement to mothers. Include fathers, grandparents, and other familiar caregivers, as well as siblings when appropriate. Provide many options so family members can choose the type and level of participation that fits their work schedules and personal preferences. For example, they can volunteer in the classroom (give them opportunities to interact with children during the daily routine, not just perform "custodial" chores), contribute materials (new and especially recycled or reusable items), attend parent meetings and workshops, write and/or receive a program newsletter, serve on advisory councils, meet with teachers formally and informally to discuss the program and their child's progress, and extend children's learning at home. Where feasible, provide transportation and child care to enable family participation in program activities.

At large-group time, David's mother brings a piñata into the classroom to celebrate his birthday. David explains to the other children, "We always have a piñata for our birthdays. We also get a cake and presents." The children all take turns hitting the piñata.

❖

At work time, Mingan uses paper and a marker, saying, "I'm writing characters. That's how my mom writes her letters." After school, the teacher asked Mingan's mom if she would like to come to small-group time the next day and write some Chinese characters with the children. She agrees and writes each child's name and other familiar words such as dog *and* book.

❖

At greeting time, Christopher reports he went to his father's workplace the day before (his father is a bus driver) and saw the new bus the drivers can use to take breaks. He says it is "clean and sparkly" and that inside is a couch and bathroom just for the drivers. When his father comes to get him at pickup time, the teachers mention how excited Christopher was about the bus and the information he shared with the class. The father says he took lots of pictures of the bus and offers to bring them in the following day. Christopher shows them off proudly, and he and two other children invent a sorting game with the pictures at work time.

Establish ties with the community

Programs often network with social services agencies to make referrals for family crises and long-term problems. However, to promote positive identity formation, programs should also establish relationships with community members who can contribute their time and caring directly to the children. Individuals and groups such as artists, tradespeople, business owners, tribal leaders, elders, and senior citizens can serve as mentors and role models. Some can host visits at their workplaces, and others can interact with children in the classroom. Discuss with them ahead of time the things that interest the children in your program, and share ideas to make these exchanges hands-on and appropriately interactive for preschoolers. The more diverse these connections, the better it communicates to children that the program values and welcomes people of all backgrounds.

It is widely acknowledged that community involvement in, and support for, SEL [social-emotional learning] programs is essential for these programs to be maximally successful. The actions of the school are enhanced when it engages the wider community in its work of educating and developing the community's children (Elias et al., 1997, p. 89)

For examples of how young children express awareness of their self-identity at different stages of development and how adults can support and gently extend learning in this KDI, see "Ideas for Scaffolding KDI 7. Self-Identity." Use these ideas to carry out the strategies described in this chapter as you play and interact with the children in your program.

Ideas for Scaffolding KDI 7. Self-Identity

Always support children at their current level and occasionally offer a gentle extension.

Earlier	Middle	Later
Children may	*Children may*	*Children may*
• Identify a characteristic or characteristics of themselves (e.g., "I'm a boy"; "I have red hair"). • Express a preference (e.g., always choose the yellow toy).	• Identify characteristics they have in common with another child (e.g., "We're both boys"). • Say what they like (e.g., "My favorite color is red").	• Identify similarities and differences in their characteristics and those of others (e.g., "We're both boys but he's taller"). • Say what they like and give a simple reason why (e.g., "I like pretzels 'cause they're salty").
To support children's current level, adults can	*To support children's current level, adults can*	*To support children's current level, adults can*
• Talk with children about their characteristics (e.g., gender; age; hair, eye, or skin color; culture; language). • Notice and describe children's preferences; accept if they do not have a preference (e.g., "Elizabeth, you seem to like yellow").	• Comment on and discuss similarities in the characteristics of children in the classroom (e.g., "In our class, lots of children have brown hair"). • Comment that different people like different things (e.g., "You really like red and Elizabeth likes yellow. I like blue").	• Acknowledge the similarities and differences in the characteristics that children notice (e.g., "You're all boys. Two of you are taller; two have brown eyes"). • Comment on children's preferences (e.g., "You took lots of pretzels because you like their salty taste").
To offer a gentle extension, adults can	*To offer a gentle extension, adults can*	*To offer a gentle extension, adults can*
• Point out the characteristics of others (e.g., at a transition, say "Everyone with curly hair, put on your coat"). • Give children opportunities to state their preferences (e.g., ask "Which color will you use?").	• Ask what other similarities children observe in their own and others' characteristics (e.g., "How else are you and Tony the same?"). • Ask the reasons behind children's preferences (e.g., "Can you tell me what made you choose that one?").	• Look for opportunities to draw children's attention to how their characteristics are similar to and different from those of others (e.g., at transition say, "If you are a girl who has a brother, wash your hands"). • Acknowledge that it is okay for children to have different preferences (e.g., "You like the salty pretzels and Tina likes the sweet raisins. Different children like different things, and that's okay!").

CHAPTER 4

KDI 8. Sense of Competence

B. Social and Emotional Development
8. Sense of competence: Children feel they are competent.

Description: Children make discoveries and solve problems with an expectation of success. They believe they can acquire the knowledge or skills they need.

At small-group time, the children share their thoughts about the steps involved in planting seeds, and the teacher draws simple pictures of their ideas. After each child gets a set of materials (a cup, dirt, seeds, and a spoon), Jabiari tells his teacher, step-by-step, how he is planting his seeds in the cup. The next week, when the teacher gives each child seeds for the outdoor flower garden, Jabiari says, "I already know what to do." He digs a hole, puts in his seeds, and covers them up. "That's how it works," he says.

At work time in the block area, when David wants to make the inside of the large cardboard box dark, he says, "I know, we could use a blanket to cover the open part. That will work for sure!"

At work time in the house area, Senguele says, "I know how to spell ballerinas." She makes the sound /b/ and says, "B." Then she adds, "I can dance like a ballerina."

How Sense of Competence Develops

Feeling competent is "the belief that one can successfully accomplish what one sets out to do" (Kagan, Moore, & Bredekamp, et al., 1995, p. 16). Children who have a sense of competence, or "self-efficacy," have the confidence to handle tasks and situations with an expectation of success. They see a challenge as something to be approached rather than avoided. Even after experiencing a setback, they quickly recover their confidence and attribute failure to a lack of knowledge or skill, which they believe they can acquire. "Such an efficacious outlook fosters intrinsic interest and deep engrossment in activities," says Albert Bandura (1994, p. 71), a pioneering researcher in this field.

At outside time, Lute rides a toy bus onto the blacktop. It gets stuck on a bike. He yanks at it several times, but the bus remains caught. He then gets off the bus, separates it from the bike, and rides onto the blacktop. "Whew! That was tough," he tells his teacher. "But I did it!"

Sense of competence versus self-esteem

A sense of competence is often used interchangeably, but erroneously, with self-esteem. Many educators believe high self-esteem is related to school success, and try to reinforce it. However, psychologists say *high* self-esteem is not the same as *healthy* self-esteem (Baumeister, Campbell, Kreuger, & Vohs, 2004). Healthy self-esteem can be high, but high self-esteem is not always healthy. If self-esteem is inflated and not tied to a realistic self-appraisal, it can even lead to poor outcomes, including unreasonable risk-taking. Baumeister et al. (2004) found that children who led others into negative or dangerous behavior often had exaggeratedly high self-esteem.

By contrast, healthy self-esteem comes from a realistic sense of one's competence, and develops when adults respect children's attempts to try new things and to solve problems. Children with healthy self-esteem find satisfaction in their own efforts without needing adult approval or praise. They also acknowledge their limitations without feelings of failure or the loss of self-worth.

At work time in the toy area, as Brendan turns puzzle pieces to make them fit, he says to himself, "Me figure this out."

❖

At outside time, Trevor jumps from the middle of the slide and says, "I jumped, I really jumped. I can do it from low and middle. I can't do it from high."

❖

At work time in the art area, Bree shows Sylvia (her teacher) that she can whistle. When Bree learns that Sylvia cannot whistle, she says, "You have to keep practicing."

❖

At work time, Devon fills a cloth bag with blocks and tries to pick it up. He squats down and tries again. When the bag doesn't budge, he stands

up, shrugs, and walks over to his teacher. "Can you help?" he asks. "It's just way too heavy for me."

Adult encouragement

Although children who feel competent do not crave praise from adults, this does not mean adults are unimportant. Rather, they help children develop a healthy self-appraisal by encouraging their initiative, persistence, and ability to reflect objectively on their efforts. For example, infants who discover their action produces an effect feel a sense of self-efficacy ("If I coo, daddy coos back"). If the infant's action does not elicit a response, or worse, evokes a negative reaction from an adult, the child will not see him- or herself as capable of having a positive effect on the world.

Likewise, as toddlers and preschoolers explore a growing range of materials and activities, adult interest and encouragement supports both their intellectual development and their emerging sense of their own abilities (Meece, 1997). Peers also become increasingly important. Children whose ideas are accepted and followed by others see themselves as competent individuals with the efficacy to influence the course of events. Classroom environments that promote collaborative rather than competitive interactions promote this evolving sense of competence (Bandura, 1994). When there are no winners or losers, all children feel good about their expanding capabilities.

Casey sees a ball stuck in the fenced area by the air conditioner unit. Twice he tries to get it out, but each time he drops it. He walks away for a few minutes, then comes back and tries once more. This time he gets the ball out and throws it over the fence. He wipes his forehead and says to his teacher, "I finally got it!"

This teacher encourages a child to explore materials so the child can discover what she is capable of doing with them.

At work time in the house area, Fiona sets up a "picnic" with a blanket, dishes, and food. She invites her teacher and several children to join her. She serves food and says, "Don't eat yet. I'm in charge." They look at her expectantly and wait until she says, "Okay. It's time to eat!"

Teaching Strategies That Support a Sense of Competence

The following teaching strategies will help to promote young children's sense of competence, and prepare them to enter school ready to undertake intellectual and social challenges.

Encourage self-help skills consistent with children's abilities and developmental levels

When teaching and caring for young children, it is important to judge success by what children set out to accomplish, not by grown-up standards. Preschoolers need time to do things on their own such as getting dressed, cleaning up spills, and sharing their ideas. Adults should resist the temptation to perform or tell children how to do tasks easier, faster, or better. Letting children help themselves on their own timetable and in their own way instills a sense of "I can do it myself!" Children will get better with maturation and practice, but if they have been criticized or discouraged, they may no longer want to try to improve. Remember that the goal is not perfection, but children's beliefs in their ability to take care of their own needs. Encourage them to repeat and rehearse their skills as often as they want to achieve mastery of something that motivates them. Acknowledge how hard they are trying, and recognize each step along the road to competence in a child's self-care.

Upon entering the classroom, Rosy tells her teacher, "This is my new sweatshirt. I know how to zip now!" All through work time and outside time, she practices zipping and unzipping her sweatshirt. Sometimes it gets stuck, but seeing that Rosy persists without getting frustrated, the teacher lets her work at improving her skill. She makes a note to herself to add more clothes with zippers to the dress-up area. She also refers other children to Rosy when they need help zipping so Rosy develops a feeling of competence assisting others.

Scaffold learning by introducing the next level of challenge when children are ready to move on

Children sometimes lack the confidence to try something a little more difficult, or they may be unsure how to go about it. Adults can provide gentle encouragement and examples. Rather than giving explicit instructions, which can imply that the adult is "better" or the child is not resourceful, the teacher can offer indirect suggestions. For example, you might say, "When I have trouble putting on my shoes, I try to loosen the laces first." Well-placed hints can also help children discover solutions on their own, as in the following anecdote:

At lunch, Joey tries unsuccessfully to open his graham crackers. He frowns and sits looking at the package.

The teacher provides just enough assistance for the child to accomplish his goal by himself.

Teacher: It's hard to open.

Joey: *(Nods)* And I'm hungry!

Teacher: Show me what you did to get the box opened.

Joey: *(Tries to lift the corner of the boxtop.)*

Teacher: I wonder if there's something on the side that would be easier to open.

Joey: *(Looks at various places on the box and then sees the perforated finger hole.)* Here?

Teacher: Try poking your finger in there and see what happens.

Joey: *(After two tries, pokes his finger in and pulls back the top.)* Whew! I was afraid I'd starve to death!

Adults can also challenge children's thinking in ways that allow them to rethink their ideas. If a child draws an erroneous conclusion or has trouble performing a task, help them consider another perspective. The more children solve problems on their own, the greater their resulting sense of self-efficacy. This process is especially important for children who are easily discouraged. In the following example, by first building Austin's self-image as a competent problem-solver, his teacher is able to scaffold further learning about spatial relationships:

At work time in the block area, Austin tries several times to stack the cardboard blocks. They keep falling down. He crosses his arms over his chest and says, "I can't do it!" His teacher asks what the problem is.

Austin: My tower won't stay up.

Teacher: Did you get any of them to stack?

Austin: Up to here. *(He stacks three blocks, all the same size.)* But when I put this one on *(he adds a larger one on top)*, they all fall down.

Teacher: *(Aligns the first three blocks and puts the fourth block next to them.)* I see something different about that one *(points to last block).*

Austin: It's bigger. *(Gets a fourth block the same size as the three smaller ones and successfully stacks them.)* Hey look!

Teacher: When you made the top one the same size as the others, you got it to stay up.

A few days later as Austin is building with the blocks alongside Jill, the teacher joins them.

Teacher: Austin's tower has blocks that are all the same, but some of Jill's blocks are different.

Austin: *(Looks at Jill's tower.)* Those *(points to the two on the bottom)* are bigger.

Teacher: I wonder how you could build a tower with different size blocks.

Austin: *(Tries to add a bigger block on top of his tower. It falls down. He looks again at Jill's tower.)* I know! The big one goes on the bottom. *(He stacks one big block and two small ones.)* There. I did it!

Support children's ideas and initiatives

Encourage children to make choices and carry out their intentions, during both *individual* and *group* activities. At child-initiated times of the day, children develop confidence in their abilities when they decide where they will play, what materials they will use and how they will use them, whether they will play on their own or with others (and if so, who), and how long they will engage in an activity. They also feel validated when teachers welcome their contributions during adult-initiated activities. Encouraging children to share their thoughts and strategies with peers sends a message that their ideas are worthwhile. Referring children to one another puts the child in the role of teacher as well as learner, and further adds to feelings of competence.

At work time in the block area, Lute says, "I'm playing Fire Out." His teacher asks how Fire Out is played. Lute explains, "You have to put the fire out at the hotel." He lifts the empty Tide container and says it has chemicals inside to put the fire out. "Can you show me how it works?" his teacher asks. Lute puts a plastic tube in the box and makes "whooshing" sounds as he "sprays" chemicals on the hotel. "You put the fire out!" says his teacher. "It might start again," says Lute, who keeps guard over the hotel for the remainder of work time.

❖

At recall time, as she jumps down the row of carpet squares (each representing one area), Fern says, "I'm going to jump over the toy area." She does and smiles with satisfaction.

❖

At small-group time, Kovid identifies a dinosaur as a "duck bill." He says he can't remember its "real" name. "I wonder how you could find out?" his teacher asks. "Look it up," says Kovid. He looks in one of the dinosaur books until he finds the right picture and its name.

Acknowledge children's efforts and accomplishments

Praise can make children depend on the judgment of others, and prevent them from developing the tools to evaluate their own work (Katz, 1993; Kohn, 1993/1999). By contrast, encouragement helps children look at the knowledge and skills they are gaining with positive self-regard.

At work time in the book area, Ben gets out the firefighter puzzle that his teacher Shannon brought in after the class field trip to the fire station. He brings it to her when it's finished and says, "Tada!" Shannon says, "You look proud and excited that you put the puzzle together." Ben smiles and does the puzzle again.

To encourage rather than praise young children, teachers can use the following strategies:

- *Watch and listen.* Being quiet — paying attention with our eyes and ears — is an effective way to communicate interest and to support children's efforts.

At outside time, Chris runs and dribbles the big red ball, saying, "Look, Mrs. Freire. When the grass is right here, I can go away." She watches as he shows her how he moves the ball away from the edge and stays on the path with a continuous dribble.

- *Imitate children's actions and repeat their words.* These behaviors show that you regard what they do as evidence of their competence and that you value their ideas enough to repeat or try them yourself.

Jacey zips her coat without any help and says, "Teacher, look, I zipped my coat!" Her teacher replies, "You zipped your coat all by yourself."

- *Comment on what children do.* Comments indicate you are taking the time to observe and reflect on children's actions. It also serves as a model for them to engage in self-reflection, developing this important aspect of their thought processes.

Ashley pumps on a swing and says, "I'm making it go high by myself." When her teacher wonders how, Ashley says, "My legs go up and down and I pull my body back and up."

- *Show children's work to others, including peers and parents.* Displaying every child's work makes them all feel equally valuable and capable. It discourages comparisons and avoids situations in which children feel

This teacher listens with interest and enthusiasm to a child's idea.

disappointed or incompetent if their work is not chosen. To involve parents in supporting their children's emerging sense of competence, send work home, share it at conferences and informally, and explain what it reveals about their young child's learning.

Provide opportunities for children to be leaders

Being the leader helps children see themselves as capable people whose ideas are taken seriously by others. There are many opportunities throughout the day to acknowledge their leadership. For example, ask them to suggest ways to move at large-group time or transition between activities. Refer children to one another for help

or ideas to emphasize they have valuable lessons to share.

Children should not be forced or required to lead, but everyone who wants to lead should have the opportunity. Respect shy or reticent children who choose not to. However, they may be more willing to lead if given the opportunity rather than having to assume the role on their own. For example, ask each child if he or she has an idea rather than asking the whole group, "Who has an idea?"

When children do choose to share with the group, teachers may need to repeat or rephrase their ideas to make sure others hear and understand them. That makes it more likely their classmates will follow, and it helps children feel they are competent contributors to the classroom. Teachers may also need to give children time to think of ideas. Sometimes, in their eagerness to lead, they volunteer before they have actually thought of what they want the group to do.

As he danced to the music at large-group time, Jabiari said, "See how high I can jump!" Later, as he clapped his hands to the beat, he said, "I can clap my hands!" His teacher said, "I wonder if we can all clap our hands," and Jabiari smiled as the others took up his action.

For examples of how young children demonstrate a sense of competence at different stages of development and how adults can scaffold learning in this KDI, see "Ideas for Scaffolding KDI 8. Sense of Competence" on page 46. Use the ideas in the chart, as well as the strategies detailed here, to support and gently extend children's learning during play and other interactions.

Ideas for Scaffolding KDI 8. Sense of Competence

Always support children at their current level and occasionally offer a gentle extension.

Earlier	Middle	Later

Children may

- Assume they need adult help to do something (e.g., "I don't know how. Can you help me?").
- Explore a variety of materials and activities, unaware of their abilities (e.g., do or attempt to complete a simple puzzle).

Children may

- Try to do something but doubt their ability to succeed at it (e.g., approach hesitantly; look for help soon after trying it on their own).
- Identify what things they think they are good at (e.g., "I'm really good at puzzles").

Children may

- Try to do something either confident they can succeed or able to learn what is needed to succeed (e.g., when an adult asks, say, "No. I can do it myself!").
- Challenge themselves to attempt new or more difficult things (e.g., "I'm gonna try the big floor puzzle now. It has lots of pieces!").

To support children's current level, adults can

- Ask children how you can help them (e.g., "What would you like me to do?").
- Provide a wide variety of materials at many developmental and ability levels.

To support children's current level, adults can

- Acknowledge and express confidence in children's efforts (e.g., "You've climbed up this far. You're almost there!").
- Acknowledge children's sense of competence (e.g., "You *are* really good at doing puzzles!").

To support children's current level, adults can

- Acknowledge children's confidence in themselves (e.g., "You're sure you can do it on your own!").
- Share children's excitement and high expectations for themselves (e.g., "I'm excited you're going to try the big floor puzzle. I bet you can do it!").

To offer a gentle extension, adults can

- Break down a task or activity into simple steps (e.g., "First try to loosen the laces, then put your foot in your shoe"); offer suggestions (e.g., "Sometimes I try to turn it another way").
- Label children's accomplishments (e.g., "You stacked the blocks!").

To offer a gentle extension, adults can

- Refer children to one another for help (e.g., "Maybe Ellis can show you how he climbed to the top").
- Point out to children materials that are slightly more challenging (e.g., "These puzzles have more pieces").

To offer a gentle extension, adults can

- Encourage children to share their skills with others (e.g., "You figured out how to do it. Do you think you can show June how you did it?").
- Ask children what would make something harder and how they could master it (e.g., "What would make it heavier? Could you lift it then?").

CHAPTER 5

KDI 9. Emotions

B. Social and Emotional Development
9. Emotions: Children recognize, label, and regulate their feelings.

Description: Children identify and name their emotions, and recognize that others have feelings that may be the same as or different from their own. They regulate the expression of their feelings.

At small-group time, David draws a picture to continue the story of Harold and the Purple Crayon. He draws a circle with eyes, nose, and a frowning mouth, then draws two lines down for the legs. "Here comes the monster. He looks sad," David says. Then he draws a smiling figure and announces, "Here comes the superhero. He looks happy."

At work time in the book area, Jayla, Brianna, Ella, and Emily pretend to drive a car to California to visit their grandmas. Jayla says, "They're happy grandmas because they smile." Brianna adds, "Whenever I visit my grandma, she says, 'I am just so happy to see you!'"

At small-group time, while coloring and listening to a piece of music, Lily says to Francine, her teacher, "It's sad when no one plays with me." Francine says, "This song reminds you of feeling sad when kids don't want to play with you?" Lily shakes her head yes and says while moving her body, "I'm just showing you my sad moves so you will understand." When listening to another song and drawing with a crayon in each hand, Lily says to Francine, "This is my happy look, like going to the museum or stuff like that."

How Emotions Develop

The components of emotion

Emotional awareness is understanding that one has feelings as distinct from thoughts; identifying and naming those feelings; and recognizing that others have feelings that may be the same as or different from one's own. Developmental psychologist Susanne Denham (2006) says that young children gain emotional knowledge and skills in three areas. *Expression* is experiencing and showing emotions. Children learn how to communicate what they are feeling using facial expressions, gestures, and words. *Regulation* is the ability to control how one expresses emotions, an emerging but still difficult skill for preschoolers. Their self-control improves when they can identify and label emotions with greater accuracy; knowing, for example, when they are feeling "bad" because they are "angry" (rather than because they are feeling "sad" or feeling "bored"). *Knowledge* is understanding how emotions affect individual behavior and social relationships. Children gradually learn to better create, maintain, and respond to social situations.

Influences on emotional development

Emotional development is complex and is influenced by many factors. According to researchers Cybele Raver, Pamela Garner, and Radiah Smith-Donald (2007), four factors are particularly important. One is the innate *temperamental differences* children are born with. (See "Aspects of Temperament" on p. 6.) Some are more vulnerable to negative emotions (such as anxiety, anger, or inhibition) while others approach life more positively (they are sociable, adventurous, or drawn to novelty). *Cognition* (perception and knowledge) is also intertwined with emotion. For example, high levels of negative arousal make it difficult to focus, while positive emotions can facilitate learning. *Language development* also contributes to emotional competence by helping children name their feelings and understand the verbal content of the emotional messages that others deliver. Finally, a child's emotional learning is influenced by *socialization* such as modeling (seeing how others handle their own feelings and respond to the child's displays of emotions), depictions of emotion in the media, and explicit teaching about emotions at home, in school, and in the community and society as a whole.

At greeting circle, Amanda said, "I'm so excited! Me and daddy and Jess are going to the pumpkin patch today!"

❖

At recall time, Jibreel recounts that another child "said he was not my friend and he hurt my feelings. I'm sad."

❖

At work time in the art area, Trevor waits for a turn at the red paint pump. The child using it says to him, "Be patient." Trevor sighs and

responds, "My grandma always says, 'Hold your patience' and it just makes me get stressed."

For preschoolers, their growing vocabulary is especially useful in helping them differentiate emotional states. So is their ability to form mental representations, which allows them to imagine and act on solutions to emotionally based problems. For example, it is often easier for children to be patient if they can picture the sand timer running out and know their turn comes next. A child who is distressed by the absence of a parent can find comfort in imagining his or her return:

At outside time (before dismissal), Penina looks around, and her teacher asks what she is thinking. Penina says, "I'm thinking about mommy and how I love her. She's gonna pick me up soon."

By the time they are in preschool, children begin to be able to identify their different emotional states.

Being able to label feelings and imagine solutions not only helps children regulate emotions, it may even affect their brain development. Research on the stress hormone cortisol shows repeated trauma can hinder neural growth, while releasing feelings — for example, by labeling them and letting them go — can help children cope with intense experiences and emotions (Perry, 1994).

Children with better emotional knowledge are also more likely to form friendships and get help from adults to negotiate social relationships. Conversely, those who have trouble with emotional regulation may also be less competent at acquiring emotional knowledge. They may over-identify negative emotions, especially anger. Consider these contrasting responses of two preschoolers:

At outside time, when a child hits him, Jabiari says, "Hands on your own body. I don't like that." When the same child later hits Jabiari's friend Mac, Jabiari says to him, "Don't hit my friend." Then he walks over to Mac and asks, "Are you all right?" He puts his hand on Mac's shoulder.

At work time in the toy area, Luis and Perry play alongside one another with magnet tiles. When his magnet tile "rocket" falls apart, Luis points at Perry (who is standing two feet away) and says, "He broke it. I'm not playing anymore."

Research shows that approximately 20 percent of preschoolers may be at risk for moderate to clinically significant social and emotional difficulties, with those from low-income families at greater risk (Raver et al., 2007). Fortunately, early intervention can be very effective, provided it focuses on emotional support and modeling, rather than "explicit" instruction or coercion

about how to behave. Helping children's overall academic, social, and physical competence can also affect their emotional development. Children who feel competent and in control of events may in turn develop the cognitive skills and motivation to better regulate their emotional states. "Quite simply, happier children fare well, and angrier or sadder children worse" (Denham, 2006, p. 88).

Teaching Strategies That Support Emotions

To help young children navigate their own and others' emotions, adults can use the teaching strategies described here.

Accept children's full range of emotions as normal

Do not judge emotions as good or bad. Although you need to stop hurtful or unsafe behavior that may result from strong negative emotions (see KDI 15. Conflict resolution), children need reassurance that it is the behavior and not the underlying feelings that you are limiting. They can learn to control their responses to feelings, but they should not think they must deny the emotions themselves.

Show your acceptance of children's emotions by paying attention to them through words, facial expressions, and gestures. It is as frustrating to children as it is to adults when they share their feelings — pleasure as well as pain — and do not get any recognition in response. To let children know you have observed and considered their feelings, adults can make eye contact, remain still and patient as they get their feelings out, nod, and get down on their level.

At planning time, Gaby says she wants to make a card for her mother who is out of town. In the art area, Gaby folds a piece of blue paper vertically and asks her teacher to help her write on the inside, "I love you, Mommy." As Gaby decorates the front and back of the card, the teacher says, "It looks like you want your mommy to know you love her." Gaby replies, "Yeah, I miss her when she's gone but now she knows I love her."

Not all children can or do show emotions, depending on their personalities, family norms, and/or cultural factors. To help them develop safe and comfortable means of self-expression, accept and begin where they are. Children with emotionally restrictive backgrounds need time to develop a sense of security and learn socially acceptable ways to express themselves. Teachers should be especially gentle and patient with such children, neither pressuring them before they are ready nor overreacting, even positively,

when they do share their feelings. Sometimes, it is easier for children to express emotions indirectly, through role play, than it is to state their feelings directly. They also reveal their feelings through the plots and actions of the characters in stories they tell.

At work time in the block area, while sitting in the "puppy house," Amelia says, "Ruff, ruff, the puppy is lonely and now it's mad. It needs to go on a walk."

At breakfast, Madison turns a half-bagel so the ends point down, and says, "My bagel man has a frown. He's sad because he misses his mommy and daddy."

❖

With a hug and other body language, this teacher shows acceptance of an upset child's feelings.

At work time in the art area, Emily draws a whale and tells her teacher, "Humphrey the whale was in a trap. He wanted to go home, but he was lost and sad because he missed his mom and dad a lot. Some people were after him and he was in trouble. The parents found Humphrey the whale, but the people were still after him. The people were after the parents. Another whale was going to the deep water to save Humphrey and his mom and dad."

Teachers can also help parents understand, in respectful ways, how young children benefit from expressing feelings appropriately. If there are discrepancies between home and school, they can negotiate what is acceptable in each place. With simple explanations and support from adults, preschoolers are capable of understanding that different rules apply in different settings. It is another facet in their learning where, when, and how to express emotions.

Name or label children's emotions as well as your own

By preschool, most children have learned the words for a few basic emotions, such as "angry," "happy," and "sad." Increasingly, early childhood programs are also introducing the signs for words, including emotions, to help preverbal children (infants, toddlers) and those with hearing impairments, speech and language delays, autism, or other special needs express their thoughts and feelings (Daniels, 2001). Even preschoolers with normally developing language skills appear to benefit from using signs, not only from a social and emotional perspective, but in terms of pre-literacy skills as well. For a dictionary of American Sign Language (ASL), with video clips illustrating the signs, visit the American Sign Language Browser website.

Adults can encourage children to use the labels that are familiar to them, and then repeat them so other children can hear the words in context. It also helps to expand simple statements to clarify which labels children are attaching to the feelings and experiences they commonly encounter.

At work time, Aubrey looks in the mirror and says, "I'm happy today." Milton, his teacher, looks in the mirror so their faces show side by side. Milton smiles and says, "I'm happy too."

At planning time, when Kiley makes a plan that does not include him, Jermaine says of his friend, "I get sad when he makes bad choices." The teacher responds, "You feel sad because Kiley wants to play something different today."

At recall time, Gabrielle reports, "I was excited at the computer because I was looking at the sand timer." Her teacher, not sure what she means, asks "You were excited looking at the sand timer?" Gabrielle explains, "I didn't have to give Jalessa a turn yet. I was excited to play on the computer more."

At work time, Chad scowls and kicks the blocks when his tower falls down. His teacher makes the sign for angry ("The fingers pull away from the face to show the wrinkles on the face of the angry person," ASL Browser, 2000). Chad nods and makes the sign back to her.

As their vocabularies expand, children also begin to understand more sophisticated terms for their feelings. Teachers can introduce new words, especially those children may have heard but have not yet connected to their own emotions. If they hear these words in the context of a situation that is meaningful to them, children are more likely to add them to their own emotional vocabularies.

At greeting time, Bianca reports, "I'm glad I'm not late today. I heard the beeps in the Pepper Café when I was eating breakfast with my mom." Her teacher says, "When you heard the clock beeping, you worried you'd be late." Bianca replies, "I worried I'd miss greeting time."

Adults can also supply new words to help children deal with the feelings that are aroused by social conflicts. As described in chapter 11 (KDI 15. Conflict resolution), this is best done when emotions are not running high, for example, after a situation has been resolved. New words can also be introduced before conflicts arise, for example, while reading a book in which feelings play a central role in a character or plot. A book such as *Where the Wild Things Are* by Maurice Sendak (1963), can open up a discussion about anger or a child's fear of losing someone's love when they act "bad." If the characters' emotions are familiar, but not currently highly sensitive for the children, they can more readily process the new information and apply it later.

Finally, remember it is valuable for children to hear you label your own emotions as

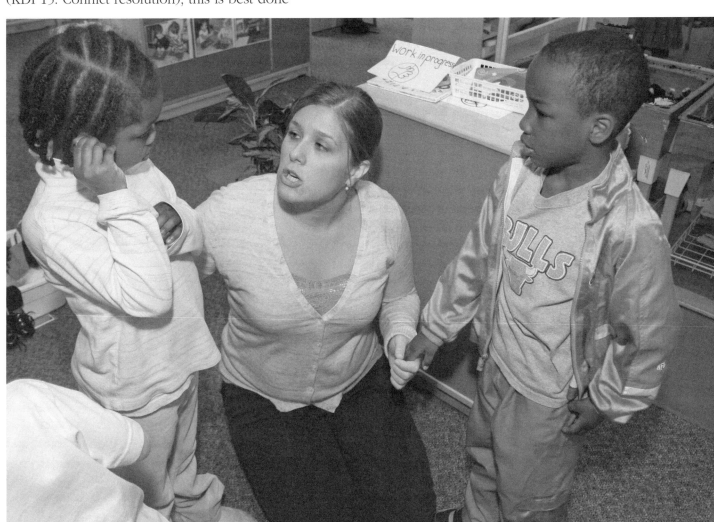

Adults help children learn to read emotional signs by interpreting children's emotions for their peers.

you interact with them throughout the day. Acknowledging and naming your feelings helps children learn that everyone has them and that the nature and range of your feelings is comparable to theirs. By seeing how you deal with your emotions — again, both positive and negative ones — children will learn how they can handle emotions with the same names and characteristics in their own experience.

At greeting circle, Max tries to tell the class it is his birthday, but the other children are not listening to him. The teacher says, "I am feeling frustrated that children are not listening to Max." Max puts his hands on his hips and says, "I am frustrated too."

Call attention to the feelings of others

Although preschoolers are increasingly able to take perspectives other than their own, they do not always do so automatically. Making them aware of the feelings of others helps them understand that emotions are universal. They also see how the expression of those feelings is the same as, or sometimes different from, their own.

Adults can also interpret children's emotions for their peers. Just as learning to read letters is part of literacy, learning to read emotional signs is part of social-emotional competence. Help children by describing emotional indicators such as body language (clenched fists, jumping for joy, walking away, gentle patting), facial expressions (grins, scowls, downcast eyes), and verbalizations (growls, yelling, angry words, soothing hums). Adult interpretation is especially useful for children who are not (yet) adept at picking up these cues themselves. It is also valuable when children are momentarily too overwhelmed or self-involved to notice others' feelings.

Comment on and discuss feelings throughout the day

Casual remarks about feelings brings them into the realm of ordinary life. The world of emotions then becomes just one of the many content areas — along with reading, mathematics, science, art, and so on — that children are learning about. Emotions that might otherwise be overwhelming do not seem as scary or unmanageable when they are part of everyday experience.

At work time in the art area, Mimi says, "My sister is so mean to me. She broke my necklace. I just can't believe it! It was my most special one! She goes to day care now." Her teacher comments, "When I was growing up, my little sister did the same thing, and it made me really angry too! I'm happy for you that your sister will have other things to play with in day care."

In conversing with children about their feelings, it is important to notice and remark on positive as well as negative emotions. For example, a range of adult comments at greeting time might include: "You look sad this morning," "What a big smile! I think you're very happy today," or "You sound excited that you played at Sally's house after school yesterday."

Because of their growing representational capacity, preschoolers can begin to talk about emotions apart from their ongoing experience. For example, children can discuss the reactions a storybook character has to a particular situation, especially if you help them relate it to situations familiar to them. Common emotion-provoking experiences and story plots include the birth of a sibling, a pet's death, going to the doctor, or the anger of a parent or friend.

When Mrs. Mel reads Where the Wild Things Are *by Maurice Sendak (1963), Chelsie asks,*

"Why is his mommy angry?" Timmy suggests it's because Max got his wolf suit dirty. Jonah offers that his mother took away his dinner because he wouldn't eat his vegetables. Mrs. Mel asks what other things might make a parent mad. The children talk about getting into fights with siblings, being "pokey" at bedtime, and not putting away their toys. When they get to the end of the book, Chelsie points to the food waiting in Max's room. "His mommy was angry, but she still loved him and gave him his dinner," says Mrs. Mel.

Art is another stimulus for expressing and talking about feelings, whether it is art the children make themselves or artwork created by others. Children enjoy looking at art and talking about the feelings behind it, including the artist's intentions and how the colors or shapes make them feel.

At small-group time, the teacher begins with a story about a boy who's mad because his friend won't play with him. The children talk briefly about what makes them angry and then use paper and crayons to represent their ideas. As they work, the children talk about angry colors, mad faces, and mad actions. One draws herself with a "mad face." Another says, "I stomped so hard I made a hole in the paper!" Another draws the "really, really red tee shirt" he wears when he is "very, very angry."

For examples of how preschoolers deal with emotions at different stages of development and how adults can support and occasionally extend learning in this KDI, see "Ideas for Scaffolding KDI 9. Emotions" on page 56. The additional suggestions offered in the chart will help you carry out the strategies already described in your daily play and other interactions with children.

Ideas for Scaffolding KDI 9. Emotions

Always support children at their current level and occasionally offer a gentle extension.

Earlier	Middle	Later

Children may

- Express emotions (e.g., cry when their shirt gets wet; smile when a parent comes to pick them up).
- Act out emotions, unaware of how they affect others (e.g., hit, kick, or bite when angry; greet other children with a bear-hug even though those children do not want to be touched that way).

Children may

- Label emotions (e.g., happy, sad, angry, worried, excited, afraid).
- Try to control how they express emotions, though not always successfully (e.g., tell another child, "Stop. I don't like it when you do that!"; grab a toy but give it back when the other child protests).

Children may

- Identify and give a reason for emotions (e.g., "I'm excited 'cause my grandma's coming!").
- Consistently control the expression of their feelings; delay gratification (e.g., say "I'm frustrated, this is hard!" instead of throwing a puzzle on the floor; follow someone else's idea first at large-group time even though they are anxious to share their idea).

To support children's current level, adults can

- Label and describe the feelings children express (e.g., "Serena is smiling. I think she looks happy").
- Help children regain control of their emotions (e.g., hold, stroke, murmur, or breathe with them).

To support children's current level, adults can

- Expand vocabulary (e.g., "Noah is afraid his mom won't be back. He's worried about being left alone").
- Acknowledge when children control their emotions (e.g., "You were angry — so you asked him to stop, and he did").

To support children's current level, adults can

- Ask children the reason why they or others feel the way they do (e.g., "You look excited today. I wonder why").
- Acknowledge when children delay gratification (e.g., "You were excited to see the doll, but you waited until Reba finished with it").

To offer a gentle extension, adults can

- Encourage children to name their feelings in their own words (e.g., "You're crying. I wonder what you're feeling").
- Point out how children's emotional expressions affect others (e.g., "Look at Sara's face. She doesn't like it when you hug her so tightly").

To offer a gentle extension, adults can

- Encourage children to share the reasons behind their emotions (e.g., "You're upset. Can you tell me why?").
- Suggest other ways children can express their emotions (e.g., "If you're excited to see Sara, you could tell her "Hi!").

To offer a gentle extension, adults can

- Ask children what would change an emotion (e.g., while reading a book, say, "She looks afraid. What would make her not be afraid?").
- Point out the beneficial effects of children delaying gratification (e.g., "Thank you for letting Evan share his idea first. It really made him happy. Now let's hear your idea").

CHAPTER 6

KDI 10. Empathy

B. Social and Emotional Development

10. Empathy: Children demonstrate empathy toward others.

Description: Children understand the feelings of others by drawing on their own experiences with the same emotions. They respond empathically by sharing the happiness of others and offering assistance when they see that others are emotionally upset or physically hurt.

At greeting circle, when Andrew looks sad after his mother leaves, Jessica walks over to give him a hug and says, "Don't worry. Your mommy's gonna come back."

Today is Connor's first day at school. At work time, he stands at the side of the room. Jamaica leaves her friends in the house area and walks over to him. "You don't have any friends, so you can play with us," she says. She takes his hand, leads him to the house area, and says, "He can be the baby." She hands him a bottle, pats his arm, and tucks a blanket around him.

At work time in the art area, Casey sees that his friend Xavier is upset and says, "Come play with me at the water table. It will help make you happy."

At work time in the block area, when Kovid crawls over Senguele's body, she starts to cry. Kovid rubs her back to comfort her. "Okay now?" he asks after a while, and she nods.

How Empathy Develops

Empathy is the ability to understand another person's feelings by experiencing the same emotion ourselves. To be empathic, we must be able to see a situation from someone else's perspective, to "put ourselves in their shoes." Seeing things from another perspective is a cognitive as well as a social-emotional skill. For example, to give directions to our house, we must think about where the other person is coming from. What differentiates empathy from other types of perspective-taking is that empathy involves emotions as well as cognitive or intellectual processes.

Piaget (1950) called this process "decentering," because it means shifting from an egocentric view of the world to taking a position outside oneself. Empathy involves imagining or forming a mental representation of how things look or feel to someone else. Preschoolers are developing this ability and can make educated guesses by projecting their own feelings onto others.

At snacktime, Dulce says that she will share her Halloween pumpkin bucket with Iva because Iva does not have one. "She might cry if nobody gave her candy."

At greeting time, while reading a book to several children, Mrs. Mel turns to the picture of Buttons McKitty being sad on a rainy day. Chelsea says, "Cats don't like to get wet." "I wonder why that is," the teacher asks. "It tickles their whiskers," says Brady, "and that feels bad. I don't like to be tickled either."

When empathy begins

Because of the complex mental processes involved, developmental psychologists debated for many years whether young children were capable of empathy. Yet research spanning over three decades (e.g., Marvin, Greenberg, & Mossler, 1976; Eisenberg, Spinrad, & Sadovsky, 2006) challenges previous notions that empathy does not appear until age seven, the beginning of concrete operations. In fact, toddlers, and even infants, exhibit early signs of empathic behavior, while empathy in preschoolers can be quite sophisticated.

For example, research reviewed in *From Neurons to Neighborhoods* (National Research Council and Institute of Medicine, 2000) shows that babies are interested in one another from at least as early as two months of age. Infants get excited by the sight of other babies and stare avidly at one another. In the middle of the first year of life, they match their behavior to the emotional expressions of significant others (for example, approaching a smiling caregiver or turning away from one who is frowning). These

Young children are capable of taking another person's perspective. This child soothes a friend who is tired and upset.

early signs of "social referencing" are a precursor of empathy and are rooted in both genetic factors, such as temperament, and environmental factors, especially parenting (Emde, 1998).

How young children display empathy

Toddlers display empathy by orienting themselves to sounds of distress, looking to see what is happening, showing emotional arousal (such as facial expressions), and doing prosocial things such as helping, soothing, or sharing (Zahn-Waxler, Radke-Yarrow, Wagner, & Chapman, 1992). They not only grasp that helping people who are hurt is important, they understand that causing hurt is bad and begin to create a rudimentary system of moral behavior.

When Kelsey, aged 20 months, sees another child frowning near the water table, she walks over to her and says, "What matter?"

By age three, preschoolers are capable of *perceptual perspective taking.* They make inferences about what others see or hear. Four-year-olds exhibit *conceptual perspective taking.* They infer other people's internal or intangible experiences such as their thoughts, desires, and feelings.

During outside time, Shawna is upset because her mother has left. Emily says, while patting Shawna's shoulder, "That's okay, your mommy will be back at outside time. When I'm sad, I make a picture for my mommy. Want to go make one for your mommy?"

According to psychologists Charles McCoy and John Masters (1985), "Young children can recognize emotions in other children, have common ideas about how experience influences affect, and are often motivated to intervene in others' emotional states" (p. 1214). They exercise these capacities because they have the ability to represent and pretend. Psychologist Paul Harris

(1989) observes that this ability "allows children to engage in an imaginative understanding of other people's mental states. Given their capacity for pretend play, children can imagine wanting something they do not actually want. They can also imagine believing something they do not actually believe. On the basis of such simple pretend premises, they can proceed to imagine the emotional reactions of another person who does have such a desire or belief" (p. 55).

Anna's cousin is visiting for the day. "I can see you're not feeling so good," Kenneth says to her at the beginning of work time. "You're new here." He gives her a "magic hat that makes you feel better."

At snack time, when Ella sees another child crying, she asks, "Is he sad because he wants his mommy?"

At work time in the house area, Anna says to Kenneth, "You're the doctor and I'm sick. You have to give me a shot. It's going to hurt a lot. I don't like to get shots."

Families are critical in developing a child's capacity for empathy (National Research Council & Institute of Medicine, 2000). Parents model empathic behavior and help children become aware of the perspectives of siblings, peers, and adults. Studies find that the more parents fulfill children's emotional needs, the better able children are to empathize with and meet the needs of others (Atance, Bélanger, & Meltzoff, 2010). However, as young children move into group care settings, their interactions with teachers and peers also influence their social perspective-taking. The cognitive skills promoted by early childhood programs further support the social skills that underlie empathy.

Teaching Strategies That Support Empathy

To support young children as they experience and express empathy, adults can use the following teaching strategies.

Model caring behavior

Preschoolers begin to learn empathy by imitating the caring behaviors of the adults around them. To create an empathic classroom, respond to the needs of children who are scared, hurt, angry, or otherwise upset. Use words, facial expressions, and body language to show you understand their feelings, and accept responsibility for helping children deal with them. To help preschoolers understand the reasons for your behavior, describe what you see and the actions you are taking.

Devon sees his teacher Hal give a teddy bear to Jason, who cries when his father drops him off. Hal holds Jason in his lap until he calms down and is ready to join others in play. The next day, Devon sees Susan crying after her mother leaves. He brings her a cuddly toy and pats her arm. They sit quietly together, then walk to the toy area and begin to work on puzzles.

At greeting time, the teacher explains to a group of children who are watching, "I'm moving over to make room for Taryn because she looks upset that she can't find a place to sit."

Individualize the type of comfort you provide based on your knowledge of what is effective for each child. Some are soothed by physical contact such as a hug or stroking. Others prefer to have a brief talk about what is bothering them. There are times when just standing nearby is all a child needs. Observe and adjust your response. Sometimes children just want their feelings recognized, while in other instances they want help solving the problem at the root of their distress.

At work time in the house area, Amelia pretends she is a cat and begins to hiss. Shannon, her teacher, asks why she is hissing. Amelia says "The kitty is scared. There's lots of sounds," and she points to the children nearby. Shannon asks what the kitty could do to be less scared. Amelia answers, "Make a 'Do Not Disturb' sign and hang it on the chair." She gets paper and markers, writes "do" and "not," and asks Shannon to help her spell "disturb." Then she tapes the sign to a chair. When the other children ask what the sign says and Amelia explains it to them, they talk in whispers. Amelia, still pretending to be a kitty, does not hiss again.

It is also important to respond positively to children who express their needs in potentially annoying or even harmful ways, such

This teacher models empathic listening with this child.

as following a teacher around, clinging to her leg, pouting silently, talking nonstop, throwing toys, or hitting. These children are seeking adult attention and reassurance, but have not yet learned more positive ways to express themselves. By responding to their needs — with understanding, patience, caring, and creativity — we can ultimately free them to engage in more satisfying interactions with adults and peers. We also show the other children in the classroom that everyone deserves compassion and caring and is capable of providing it too.

Acknowledge and label the feelings that children have in common

Although preschoolers are capable of empathy, they are still bound up in their own emotions. Adults can help them become aware that others share these feelings. Be concrete. Focus on the situation and the fact that others have the same emotions under similar circumstances. Young children can then understand and even anticipate others' responses by recalling their own experiences.

At outside time, the teacher says, "Claudia, you are frustrated because you want a turn on the swings but other children are on them. This might be how Tommy felt when he was waiting for you to finish your turn at the computer during work time."

Children are most likely to feel empathy in response to people with whom they are close. When these significant others include those who provide the care they depend upon, such as parents and caregivers, it is not uncommon for the child's own anxiety to trigger an empathic response:

At work time in the writing area, Aubrey asks her teacher to help her write on a card she is making

for her daddy, "I hope you don't get a cold like Mommy and me."

At message board, Mr. Brian (a teacher) tells the children that Miss Natalie (the other teacher) will be out sick that day. At work time, Nicholas makes her a get-well card.

Mr. Brian: You drew her head.

Nicholas: And a heart.

Mr. Brian: What does the heart mean?

Nicholas: I made Miss Natalie a heart because I'm so sad and I hope she feels better.

Children are also more likely to show compassion toward friends with whom they regularly play than toward other peers. They not only express concern about playmates who are ill or upset, they may also display remorse if they feel responsible for a friend's distress. In such cases, apologies (saying "I'm sorry") can be spontaneous and genuine, because they are not coerced by adults.

At work time in the art area, Shelby uses tape, scissors, paper, and muffin cups to make a card for her friend Abby, who is having surgery that day. Her teacher comments, "You used four different things to let your friend in the hospital know you're thinking about her." "I hope she will be okay," says Shelby, "because I know she wants to come back and play with me."

While carrying his paint cup to the sink, Quentin drips some on Daryl's sneaker. "My new shoes," Daryl cries, upset. "I'm sorry," says Quentin. "I'll wipe it off." He uses a wet paper towel to wipe off the paint. "Now your mommy won't be mad you got your shoe dirty."

As they become more aware of their different emotional states, children share their feelings with each other.

Create opportunities for children to act with empathy

Like other social and emotional skills, learning to feel empathy takes practice. Create situations where children are explicitly encouraged to listen and think about the feelings of others. For example, suppose the message board says a child is out sick on a day the class is taking a field trip to the pumpkin patch. Invite the children to choose a pumpkin for the child who isn't there, thus encouraging them to think about someone they know who is having a different experience.

Another strategy for developing empathy is to encourage children to assist one another,

for example, to hold a cup steady while another child pours, bend to pick up something dropped by a child in a wheelchair, or help a child who asks how to write his name. By encouraging all children to be helpful, without differentiating providers or recipients by age or ability level, adults help children accept that everyone needs — and can offer — assistance. Taking care of plants and animals can also help children appreciate how their actions affect the survival and well-being of others.

At work time, Malika tells her teacher, "I'm worried about Fuzzball [the class guinea pig]. I think someone forgot to feed him yesterday." When the teacher asks what makes her think so, Malika answers, "He's just sleeping all morning. He's hungry, tired and hungry." Malika puts food and water in the guinea pig's dish. "Eat up," she whispers to him, "I got it just for you." She keeps quiet watch over the cage another 10 minutes, until the animal wakes up and eats and drinks. Malika runs to her teacher and says excitedly, "Fuzzball is okay now!"

Practice perspective-taking in nonsocial situations

Since adopting other viewpoints is the cognitive basis of empathy, introduce perspective-taking activities that involve objects and actions as well as people. For example, science activities can encourage children to explore things from different angles. At outside time, ask children what they notice about a bush when they stare straight at it, look up from the ground, or gaze down from the climber. Gathering data, a mathematics activity, highlights differences of opinion. Making a chart about favorite colors reveals that some children like red, others are partial to blue or green, and some have no preference. Reading presents many opportunities for perspective-taking. Talk about what characters are thinking and feeling, or what they see or hear from various locations in the story.

Looking at a book of farm animals, Ben says, "These are inside the barn and those are outside. The other ones want to get inside." When his teacher asks how they could get inside, Lily pipes up, "They can't because the outside ones are wild." Ben says, "The farmer could adopt them." Lily thinks this over. "Then the inside ones could have brothers and sisters."

Being the leader in movement activities also helps preschoolers consider other perspectives. When they give directions using words, rather than just demonstrating what to do, they have to put themselves in the place of those receiving instructions. For example, it may be observable that the child who is leading is bending down, so the others imitate this movement. However, if the leader specifically wants them to touch their toes, he or she will have to say so to be clear.

Finally, many art activities involve perspective-taking. When children build structures with three-dimensional materials, encourage them to view it — even take photos — from many angles. As children look at artwork, ask them to consider what the artist wanted to say or why he or she chose certain materials. These discussions not only encourage children to reflect on the perspectives of the maker and viewer, they can also tap into the feelings that art evokes, furthering the foundations of social understanding.

At work time in the art area, Monique paints a blue sky with a white streak in it and calls it a "jet stream." She tells her teacher, "Jets fly over my house upside down and sideways. Pilots can't see me when they're upside down." Her teacher asks what they do see. Monique replies, "I think they see God up there."

For examples of how young children express empathy at different stages of development and how adults can scaffold learning in this KDI, see "Ideas for Scaffolding KDI 10. Empathy." The ideas suggested in the chart will help you support and gently extend young children's capacity for empathy as you play and otherwise interact with them throughout the program day.

Ideas for Scaffolding KDI 10. Empathy

Always support children at their current level and occasionally offer a gentle extension.

Earlier	Middle	Later

Children may

- See only their own perspective in play situations (e.g., sit in the middle of another child's train track because they want to play with the blocks on the nearby shelf).
- Be aware of another child's emotions; may ask adult the reason (e.g., stop what they are doing to look at a child who is excited or upset; ask the teacher "Why is she laughing?" or "Why is he crying?").

Children may

- Label the perspective of others (e.g., Landon notices Matthew just sitting on the swing and tells the teacher that Matthew needs a push).
- Exhibit caring behavior in response to another child's emotions (e.g., laugh with another child; bring a teddy bear to a crying child).

Children may

- Adapt what they are doing based on their understanding of someone else's perspective (e.g., Abby stops splashing at the water table when Joshua says it's getting his hair wet).
- State why they showed caring behavior to another child (e.g., "I hugged her because it's her birthday"; "I brought Theo the teddy bear because he misses his mommy").

To support children's current level, adults can

- Label and explain children's own perspectives to them (e.g., "You chose to go to the block area because you really like building things").
- Label other children's emotions (e.g., "You're excited because your grandma is coming for dinner tonight").

To support children's current level, adults can

- Explain others' perspectives (e.g., "Joey also wants a turn at the computer").
- Acknowledge when children exhibit caring behavior (e.g., "You saw Alec was crying, so you helped him wipe up the spilled paint").

To support children's current level, adults can

- Acknowledge when children adapt their behavior based on another's perspective (e.g., "Justin, you moved to make room for Caprice").
- Provide opportunities for children to explain their caring behavior (e.g., "Alicia, you gave Tommy a hug. I'm wondering why").

To offer a gentle extension, adults can

- Call attention to similarities and differences among children's perspectives (e.g., "Kailee also likes to do puzzles. You like to do the big floor puzzles; she likes to do the wooden puzzles").
- Model and label caring behavior (e.g., "Chelsea had a lot of blocks to clean up so I offered to put some away").

To offer a gentle extension, adults can

- Look for opportunities to connect other children's perspectives with possible actions (e.g., "It looks like Mikey is trying to carry the heavy tire up the hill. He could probably use more people to help him").
- Look for opportunities to encourage children to exhibit caring behavior (e.g., "It looks like the fish need to be fed. They get hungry like us. I wonder what we could do").

To offer a gentle extension, adults can

- Help children anticipate the perspective of others (e.g., "Anna broke her arm. It's in a cast and she needs to keep it very still. What can we do when she comes back to help keep her arm safe?").
- Encourage children to recall and describe similar situations and the feelings they evoked (e.g., "Do you remember when you were little? How did you feel about going to the top of the climber?").

KDI 11. Community

B. Social and Emotional Development
11. Community: Children participate in the community of the classroom.

Description: Children act as members of the classroom community by participating in routines, cooperating with social expectations, and sharing responsibility for maintaining the classroom.

While getting ready for outside time, Max helps Kayla put on her tennis shoes. "Now we can all go outside quicker," he tells the teacher.

During work time, Martin is playing between the cubbies when a parent volunteer says to him, "I'm worried someone will get hurt back here." Martin stops playing and replies, "I will make a stop sign so other children know they should not play here too."

After Ella finishes her turn to recall, she says, "Then it's Matthew's turn, then Joseph's turn, then we go wash our hands, then we eat snack."

After painting at small-group time, Isaac washes his hands, cleans off his place at the table, sees that Roxanne has completed her painting, and cleans off her place too.

At the end of outside time, as Carmella, the last child to be picked up, sees a tricycle left on the playground. She tells her mother to wait while she stores it inside the shed, and says, "Now it will stay dry until tomorrow."

Having a sense of community means seeing oneself as belonging to the group and sharing many of its characteristics, beliefs, and practices. The early childhood classroom is a community whose members share an age range, activities, interests, time, and friendship. The members receive and give one another individual and group support. Through their interactions in this community, and its shared expectations for behavior, young children also deepen their understanding of broader social norms and conventions.

At snacktime, when David's mother brings cupcakes for everyone, Nevaeh brings a chair from the book area to the table so David's mother can sit down.

Educator Nancy Meltzoff (1994) offers weaving as a metaphor for the structure and function of the classroom community. Each individual strand, such as the common environment, shared leadership, communication, and cooperation, interacts with all the others to form an integrated whole. If one element is missing, or becomes frayed, the whole system can unravel.

But when all the components are present and smoothly interlocked, the community provides beauty, warmth, and protection, just as a well-constructed cloth does for its wearer.

How Community Develops

Community and well-being

Psychologists agree that being part of a community is necessary to a person's well-being. "The absence of a sense of belonging to a community may have a deep effect on a child's development socially and neurologically" (Katz & McClellan (1997, p. 17). Because young children are essentially social creatures, communities are meaningful and attractive to them. Membership begins with their parents and the groups their families belong to. The early childhood program is usually their first community outside this primary core. Preschoolers want to be part of this new community. However, joining it is a learning experience. Understanding its norms, and balancing their own and others' needs, are abilities that are just beginning to emerge during this period.

Paradoxically, adults can build on the natural egocentrism of preschoolers to ease them into the community. This happens when children realize the group can meet their individual needs to feel validated, competent, and important as individuals. Preschoolers make the bridge from "me" to "we" by contributing to the group and collaborating with peers who have equal status. They learn that paying attention to and negotiating with others can be personally gratifying. These are skills children cannot learn individually (Battistich, Solomon, & Watson, 1998). They must come face to face with other perspectives to understand, resolve, and integrate themselves into the group. They also depend upon adults to point out shared opportunities to achieve their individual goals.

At work time, walking by the sand table, Ashley sees sand on the floor. She says to her teacher, "Someone might fall. But it's too much to clean up myself!" Her teacher asks how she could solve the problem. Ashley answers, "I could get someone to help me" and suggests Veronica. When the teacher asks her, "What do you think she'll say?" Ashley sees Veronica is engrossed at the easel and might not want to interrupt her painting. Then her eyes light upon Solomon, who is watching a group of children in the block area. "Hey, Solomon," Ashley calls. "Wanna help me clean up all this sand?" Solomon races to get the broom and dustpan. He holds the dustpan while Ashley sweeps. They play together at the sand table for the rest of work time.

Feelings of responsibility

Beyond a respect for other individuals, part of establishing a sense of community is cultivating feelings of responsibility for the classroom as a whole. Developmental psychologists Rheta DeVries and Betty Zan (1994) say adults often underestimate the amount of responsibility young children are willing and able to accept. Since they use the classroom's materials and furnishings every day, children can observe what happens when these resources are not well cared for. For example, they can see that markers dry up when the tops are not replaced, that toys or materials get lost if not returned to their places, or that someone gets hurt when a spill is not wiped up. Tied to concrete examples, preschoolers can understand the implications of their actions — for others as well as for themselves — and alter their behavior with a mental image of the consequences and associated feelings in mind. The cognitive capacity for connecting cause and effects thus helps to create the social phenomenon we call community.

At outside time, Matthew sees the teacher sweeping rocks off the sidewalk. He goes to the shed to get a shovel and starts to push the rocks off the sidewalk too.

Teaching Strategies That Support Community

Arranging the classroom to promote interactions, and implementing a shared and consistent daily routine, help create a sense of community (see general teaching strategies, in chapter 2). The following additional practices also enable preschoolers to become members of the classroom community.

Create an atmosphere that fosters mutual respect and responsibility

The emotional tone of a classroom is the environment in which all areas of learning — affective, academic, physical, and creative — take place. Jan Randolph and Pansy Gee (2007) at the Center for Education at Rice University say a positive community sets the stage for each child to feel good about school and be a successful learner. When children feel safe, loved, and accepted, they feel connected to the learning community, including the adults and peers who share it.

In a supportive community, children assume responsibility for taking care of one another. While this involves empathy (see KDI 10. Empathy), community-mindedness goes beyond understanding someone else's feelings. One can empathize with others without being motivated to act on their behalf. A sense of community, by contrast, involves actions as well as feelings. It means helping individual members so the group as a whole can feel good and function as a unit. To do this, children must be aware of what their classmates need or want to achieve personal

goals. They must also realize that assisting one individual can benefit the larger group.

At work time in the art area, Ashley overhears the teacher say that Ben is looking for the book, "Monkeys Jumping on the Bed." Ashley stops what she is doing, goes to the book tub, pulls out the book, and gives it to the teacher. "Here's the book Ben wants," she says.

As the class gets ready for outside time, Casey sees Noam trying to snap his snow pants. He walks over and says, "Want me to do it?" Noam answers, "Yes," and Casey snaps his pants for him. "We're all ready," Casey tells his teacher. "Now we can all make snow angels."

The teacher's behavior sets the tone for the whole classroom. Thus, although it should go without saying, it is still important to state unequivocally: Adults should never shame or humiliate students, blame them in front of others, or criticize their personal attributes (appearance, intelligence, background, and so on). When children make mistakes — which they do because they have not yet learned how to behave differently — adults should use social problem-solving techniques that strengthen personal relationships, allow children to learn by working through problems, and build their sense of competence and self-esteem (Zeiger, 2007; see also KDI 15. Conflict resolution).

A regular cleanup time also helps to establish the sense of respect and responsibility that defines a community. When children participate in the designated time for cleanup, they pool their efforts to make the classroom a smoothly functioning environment. Having everyone pitch in creates a sense of ownership and shared responsibility for the equipment and materials.

The classroom belongs to the children, not just the teacher (Zeiger, 2007).

At work time in the block area, Aubrey walks up to Ms. Bev and asks her, "When it's cleanup time, can I turn the lights out? Then everyone will know it's time to put things away."

"I don't hide under the climber when it's cleanup time anymore," Jason says to Betsy. "I like to clean up. I pretend I'm a cleaner dog or a steam shovel or something."

Finally, remember that listening may be the single most important component in establishing a supportive community — not only how adults listen to children, but also how children listen to one another. To feel supported, children must know their needs and ideas are being heard and their contributions to the community are being acknowledged. Adults should also express their own pleasure at being part of a classroom in which everyone is treated with kindness and respect.

Call attention to activities the whole class participates in

Daily whole-class activities include large-group time, greeting circle, transitions, cleanup time, and outside time. Children may not be aware of the "togetherness" of these periods, but pointing them out helps children become conscious of the fact that everyone is participating as a group. In addition to activities that are routine ("We got everything put away at cleanup so we can find them tomorrow at work time"), teachers can also call attention to special activities that everyone looks forward to and shares, such as field trips ("Look at all the shells we gathered at the beach. I wonder what we can do with them") and holiday celebrations ("I wonder if we'll all

When adults really listen to children, they provide the foundation for a supportive community and help children learn to listen to each other.

recognize one another tomorrow in our Halloween costumes").

A concrete way to support children's awareness of whole-group activities is to take photos and write simple captions. These can be posted on the wall or put in a class album in the book area. In talking about the photos, or recalling class activities in general, teachers can further instill the notion of community by using phrases such as "our class," "all of us," "our group," and "all together." These simple words, heard repeatedly, communicate the unity of the group.

While communities often emerge spontaneously (e.g., "the block builders"), they also need to be consciously created and nurtured. Certain parts of the daily routine, such as large-group time, are obviously conducive to promoting a sense of community. However, other whole-class activities can also help to build an awareness and appreciation of how the group functions as a whole.

At large-group time, these children practice signing and moving along with a supportive adult.

For example, greeting time, reading the message board, or having a group problem-solving discussion are activities that bring children together. Adults can use these communal times to inform children about upcoming events or new materials. The children can contribute their own hypotheses about a "mystery" symbol on the message board, talk about something everyone is looking forward to (such as a field trip the next day), or offer solutions for a common and recurring classroom social problem (cleanup is taking a very long time). The satisfaction of dealing with issues as a group ("We solved the problem!") further builds the children's sense of belonging to a vital and meaningful community.

Bria races into the classroom, telling her teacher, "I brought a book to read. My Mom read it to me. Now you read it to my friends!"

Raphael guesses the picture on the message board means there are new markers in the art area. He and Viktor make a plan to use the markers to "make a sign for our garage" and accept Susan's offer to help them tape it up. Over the next few days, several children use the new markers to make signs (tea café, monster cave, skate store). The following week, the class takes a walk to look at the signs on their block.

To address a recurring problem over sharing, a teacher shows a small group of preschoolers a picture of two children pulling on a garden hose. They talk about what is happening and agree the children are angry. The teacher writes down their suggestions to solve the problem: share

it; take turns; give it back and forth; ask for it ("Could I have please have that?"); and both quit and do something else. The children are engaged in the discussion (despite several interruptions) and feel good about all the solutions they proposed. (Evans, 2002, pp. 259–263)

While planning such whole-group activities is important in creating community, peer interaction should never be "over-organized" or forced (DeVries & Zan, 1994). Sometimes teachers try to push it (for example, by assigning rotating play partners), especially among children who rarely interact with others. Although well-intentioned, such coercion can actually operate against a child's sense of belonging. Whether and how to participate in activities with others should always be optional. The teacher's role is not to force or require it, but rather to create the supportive circumstances that make group activities something each child can look forward to joining.

Involve children in the community outside the classroom

Preschoolers are becoming aware of the community beyond their homes and classrooms, including the neighborhoods where these are located and other places they often visit (such as the library, parks, shopping malls, or movie theaters). Teachers can validate these experiences by showing interest and encouraging children to share them with classmates through conversations and role-playing. Bringing outside activities and familiar materials from these places into the classroom helps children become aware that they and their families are participating in the life of the community around them.

At work time in the block area, while playing dog show, Lute says to his teacher Sue, "The 'mission is free." She replies, "The admission is free." Lute explains that means you don't have to pay. Sue asks if his family had to pay when they went to the dog show the day before. "No," says Lute, "Monarch [his aunt's dog] was in the circle so we got free tickets." He tells Sue how the hair spray made his mother cough so they had to leave early. "We got DQ and then we drove to the park and I saw the ducks," he says. "You went lots of places in the city yesterday," Sue comments. "Yes," says Lute.

In addition to doing things with their families, preschoolers are also ready to join in activities that connect them to the wider community. They can participate in projects such as recycling classroom materials (see KDI 58. Ecology). A neighborhood walk can draw their attention to how residents decorate the buildings where they live and what shopkeepers display in storefronts. Children can talk about similarities and differences in their own homes and the places their families frequent.

You can also expand a child's sense of community by visiting local establishments such as the public library or farmers' market, and taking part in activities such as street fairs and parades that feature local culture (food, art, music, dance). Clip newspaper photos of familiar people, places, and events, write simple captions, and post them near the door so children and families can see and discuss them at dropoff and pickup times. In addition to venturing outside, invite guests into the classroom. Playing "hosts" reflects children's sense of ownership in their classroom community, a place where they know where things are and when things happen.

For examples of how children demonstrate membership in the classroom community at different stages of development and how adults can support and gently extend their learning, see "Ideas for Scaffolding KDI 11. Community" on page 74. These ideas will help you carry out the strategies described here during your daily play and interactions with young children.

Ideas for Scaffolding KDI 11. Community

Always support children at their current level and occasionally offer a gentle extension.

Earlier	Middle	Later
Children may	*Children may*	*Children may*
• Watch parts of the daily routine from the sidelines (e.g., stand apart and watch children move on the rug at large-group time).	• Join in classroom routines (e.g., clean up after work time and go to the table for lunch; sign in when they arrive).	• Know what part of the routine comes next; comment on exceptions (e.g., "After recall, we eat snack"; "Today we're going for a walk instead of playing on the swings").
• Engage in activity independent of classroom expectations (e.g., start to take toys off the shelf at large-group time).	• Follow classroom social expectations (e.g., listen while another child talks at large-group time; take only two crackers at snacktime so there's enough left for others).	• Remind other children of classroom expectations (e.g., tell another child after snack, "Joey, put your cup in the tub").
• Take care of their own belongings (e.g., hang up their coat; put their artwork in their cubby).	• Help to maintain the classroom (e.g., take part in cleanup, sometimes needing reminders; throw paper in the trash).	• Notice when something in the classroom needs attention (e.g., "This wheel is broken. You better ask Joe to fix it!").
To support children's current level, adults can	*To support children's current level, adults can*	*To support children's current level, adults can*
• Provide nonverbal encouragement (smile, nod) for children to join if/when they are ready but never force them to participate.	• Acknowledge when children join routines (e.g., "You knew it was small-group time, so you came to the table").	• Encourage children to anticipate what comes next in the routine.
• Explain expectations; offer choices (e.g., "It's large-group time. We stay on the rug. You can either sing with us or sit and listen").	• Acknowledge when children follow classroom expectations on their own (e.g., "Thanks for leaving some juice for Pedro").	• Note when children remind one another of classroom expectations (e.g., "You helped Joey remember what to do with his cup after snack").
• Acknowledge when children take the initiative to care for their own belongings (e.g., "You hung up your coat").	• Provide opportunities for children to help maintain the classroom (e.g., wash the snack table; store bikes after outside time).	• Acknowledge when children notice something in the classroom needs attention (e.g., "It's a good thing you told me it was broken before someone got hurt").
To offer a gentle extension, adults can	*To offer a gentle extension, adults can*	*To offer a gentle extension, adults can*
• When an activity is underway, invite children to participate.	• Involve children in giving warnings and/or signaling transitions.	• Encourage children to share the routine with one another, parents, and visitors.
• Talk with children about the next part of the routine just before a transition (e.g., "Next it will be small-group time, and you can go to your table").	• Offer a simple explanation for social expectations (e.g., "In our classroom, we make sure everyone has some juice").	• Ask about the reason behind expectations (e.g., "I wonder why it's important to listen to one another at large-group time").
• Encourage children to begin to help take care of classroom materials (e.g., "Can you put this doll back in the cradle?").	• Acknowledge when children take responsibility without being reminded ("You cleaned your paint brushes before you went to play with the blocks").	• When appropriate, involve children in attending to a classroom issue they identified (e.g., "How could we repair the torn pages in the book?").

CHAPTER 8

KDI 12. Building Relationships

B. Social and Emotional Development
12. Building relationships: Children build relationships with other children and adults.

• •

Description: Children relate to others in the classroom. They refer to teachers and peers by name. Children develop friendships, seek out others, and engage in give-and-take interactions.

At work time in the block area, Sandra says she is building a "puppy shop." Amelia, Ashley, and Ben are her puppies. Sandra says, "I give free things out." She then feeds the dogs free "Popsicles."

At planning time, Jayla says she is going to work in the art area. Then she says, "Wait. I want to talk to Ella about her plan." She finds Ella in the house area and comes back to the table to change her plan. "Ella and me are going to cook soup together in the house area," she says.

At outside time, Moya and Liam play a chase game with Rachel (their teacher). When Liam locks Rachel up in jail, Moya helps the teacher escape by pretending to unlock the jail cell. Moya then becomes a police officer with Liam, and together they chase Rachel around the playground to put her back in jail.

At small-group time, Keifer is using the pig puppet. He turns the puppet to face Shannon (his teacher) and says to her, "Oink goes the pig. When he gets scared, he sprays stinky stuff."

At work time in the art area, Felipe, Maggie, and Lara play "pizzeria." Felipe asks Shannon (a teacher), "What do you want?" She says she wants a pizza with mushrooms and lots of peppers. "Coming right up," says Felipe. He makes a pizza with play dough and beads, while Maggie and Lara mix cake batter. "Here you go," Felipe says, delivering the pizza and cake to Shannon.

Child care or preschool is often a young child's first opportunity to establish relationships beyond their home and extended kinship networks. Bolstered by the family bonds they have experienced in their earliest years, and by their growing sense of trust, autonomy, and initiative, preschool children seek and value these outside relationships. Many youngsters talk proudly about "going to school" and are eager to tell parents and other family members about their growing social circle.

How Building Relationships Develops

According to developmental psychologist Willard Hartup (1986), preschoolers are motivated to initiate and maintain "social relations with other children (a special challenge of this period), as well as effective, nondependent interactions with preschool teachers (another special challenge of the period)" (p. 15). Their ability to establish these relationships is important for several reasons. First, the program becomes a place where the child wants to spend time. Additionally, human connections provide an important context for all kinds of learning — cognitive, creative, and physical, as well as social. Early relationships also guide children's later interactions with teachers and fellow students when they begin formal schooling. Children who get along well with others adjust better and have higher achievement than those who have difficulty establishing and maintaining satisfying social relationships (Ladd, Birch, & Buhs, 1999).

Relationships among children

The relationships that preschoolers form with their peers provide many benefits: emotional support in unfamiliar settings, opportunities to play with a partner, and experiences in leading, following, making suggestions, trying out ideas, and negotiating social conflicts. As Hartup and Moore (1990) state, "considerable evidence suggests that peer relations contribute positively to mental health, both in childhood and later on. The elements in child-child relations believed to be responsible for these contributions are the developmental equivalence of children and their companions and the egalitarian nature of their interaction" (p. 2).

As early as age two, children show peer preferences (indicate who they would rather play with) and begin to form friendships (a

Sometimes friends are more likely to get into social conflicts than children who are not friends.

Young children's relationships give them opportunities to play with partners and practice leading and following, making suggestions, trying out ideas, and problem solving.

voluntary, two-way, positive bond). Friendships are unique — even toddlers adjust their style of play to each friend. The more two children play together, the greater the complexity and compatibility of the play. Toddler friendships are often sustained into preschool and preschool friendships are often multiyear (Ladd, Herald, & Andrews, 2006).

During the preschool years, relationships with peers become more reciprocal, and friendships grow more exclusive (Rubin, Bukowski, & Parker, 2006; Vandell, Nenide, & Van Winkle, 2006). Children also learn they can have more than one friend at a time. Play between friends becomes more complex, positive, and affectionate. Preschoolers also have the conceptual and verbal ability to reflect on and describe their friendships, including their reasons for liking friends, such as shared interests and desirable traits such as being funny or kind. Likewise,

they can identify the behaviors that work against forming friendships.

Destiny says, "I plan to go to the block area with Caitlin, Matthew, and Tia because we need to build our big castle. Then we'll have a queen, a princess, and Matthew can be the king we need. I like Matthew cause he always wants to play king."

At work time in the house area, when Dosia grabs a toy she is using, Alpha says, "Dosia's not my friend, and I don't play with her anymore. She's mean and she always takes our toys."

At the same time that friends get along, there can also be greater conflict than in interactions with nonfriends. This is due to more frequent contact — and thus more opportunities for conflict — between friends, as well as the fact that emotional investment between friends is higher and interactions are more intense. By late preschool, however, friends are more likely to negotiate, disengage before conflicts escalate, and work to maintain the friendship. This shift is because preschoolers become more psychologically aware of the importance of these relationships in their lives.

Relationships with adults

Children's relationships with teachers and caregivers continues to be important during preschool, just as it was in infancy and toddlerhood. However, the nature of this relationship changes. Preschoolers become more selective in the kinds of interactions they seek from adults, whether it is being comforted when they are hurt or upset, getting help to complete a task or resolve a social conflict, sharing an exciting discovery, finding a willing and responsive play partner, or simply enjoying an interesting conversation. These connections with significant adults contribute positively to young children's sense of competence and well-being, as long as the adults understand and respect children's levels of development, permit them to function as active learners, and share control rather than trying to dominate children. (For more on establishing and maintaining supportive adult-child relationships, see chapter 2.)

Adults in HighScope programs strive to have real conversations with children.

Conversing With Children: Adult Strategies

• Look for natural opportunities for conversation.

• Join children at their level for conversation.

• Respond to children's conversational leads.

• Converse as a partner with children.

  – Stick to the topic the child raises.

  – Make comments that allow the conversation to continue without pressuring the child for a response.

  – Wait for the child to respond before taking another turn.

  – Keep your comments fairly brief.

• Ask questions sparingly.

  – Ask questions that relate directly to what children are doing.

  – Ask questions about the child's thought process.

— Handler (2001, p. 37)

Teaching Strategies That Support Building Relationships

In addition to the general strategies for supporting positive interpersonal relationships described in chapter 2 and earlier in this chapter, the following teaching practices will help young children build positive and satisfying associations with adults and peers.

Interact with children in a genuine and authentic manner

According to psychologists Alan Sroufe and June Fleeson (1986), "early relations forge one's expectations concerning relationships. Expectations are the carriers of relationships" (p. 68).

When adults treat children with warmth and respect, children assume others will do the same, and these expectations can become a self-fulfilling prophecy.

At work time in the house area, when Victoria (a teacher) says her bear figure is hungry, Dante pinches a piece of play dough from his pile and tells Victoria it's a Teddy Graham for the bear.

At work time at the sand table, Mona calls Hillary (a teacher) over and says, "Will you play with me?" Hillary says yes and kneels down beside her. Mona then begins to make sand cupcakes for Hillary and Frank (another teacher).

At outside time, Penina takes the hand of Shari (her teacher) and says, "I want to play with you." Penina and Shari run away from the "police" who want to put them in jail.

Building good relationships with children does not happen automatically. HighScope preschool teachers reflect on their interactions with children not only to make sure they are positive but also to ensure they are genuine. Adults strive to have real conversations with children, rather than exchanges that are mechanical or managerial. They call children by name. Instead of bombarding children with questions or orders, they listen to what children have to say and respond appropriately, much as they would when having a conversation with an adult. Children sense this respect and respond in kind in their interactions with adults and peers.

Genuine conversations are not didactic or contrived. They happen when adults place themselves at children's physical level, listen carefully to what children are saying, give children control of conversations, accept children's pauses and

Making the Case for Stability

Carollee Howes (1987, 1988), an educational researcher who has conducted an extensive study of children's early social relations, makes a strong case for the role of stable communities in enabling children to build the relationships that help them develop social competence. Consider the following statements she has made on the subject:

> "Children who form secure attachments to their caregivers would, all else being equal, be expected to be more socially competent with their peers....The child who experiences a series of unstable caregivers may lose interest in and motivation to engage in the social world. Since social interest in the peer partner represents an early task in the development of social competency with peers, the child who experiences caregiver instability may be at risk for poor peer relationships" (Howes, 1987, p. 157).

> "The stability of the peer group increases in importance as children develop specific friendships. Particular relationships with peer partners are based on the continued presence of the partner" (Howes, 1987, p. 159).

> "The preschool children in this study received higher sociometric ratings if they had more experience with particular peers. This suggests that experience with particular peers also may contribute to the development of social skills in preschool children" (Howes, 1988, p. 57).

> "The stability of the friendships in this sample suggests that children who have sustained intimate experiences with the same peers may receive emotional support from them. Children who have maintained a large proportion of their friendships appeared to be more socially competent than children who lost their friends through separation" (Howes, 1988, p. 67).

---

nonverbal utterances, and learn and remember each child's particular interests. They are also facilitated when adults give children specific feedback, ask honest questions (those the adult does not know the answer to), and respond honestly to children's questions.

Child: That tower has a light!

Adult: I see. I wonder why it's on.

Child: It's a little bit sprinkling.

Adult: It's on because something is sprinkling.

Child: It's sprinkling. It's wet.

Adult: Oh, the light is on when it's wet.

Child: *(Makes rainlike motions with fingers.)*

Real conversations happen when children are engaged by the topic. This does not mean children must initiate the conversation, but adults should nevertheless follow their interests and leads. Psychologists and educators David

Wood, Linnet McMahon, and Yvonne Cranstoun (1980) report that children prolong conversations about the past, striking events, happy memories, speculations about the future, why events happen they way they do, and why people are the way they are. The secret to these dialogues seems to be a "sense of shared quest, in which both adult and child participate actively in the experience. The quality of sharing is signaled by the adult's readiness to express interest, surprise, and suggestions as to what is going on" (p. 189).

Maintain a stable group of children and adults

Building relationships takes time. Children, like adults, get to know others through daily interactions and meaningful contact. They learn about their own interests and what they are like as people, whether they are quiet or talkative, take things slowly or rush full speed ahead, prefer a smile or a hug (or both), or tend toward the serious or silly. To give children the time they need to form relationships, HighScope programs maintain stable groupings — the same adult and group of six to ten children — for small-group activities. So, for example, one adult meets with the same small group of children for planning and recall, small-group time, and snacktime. In this way, a child gets to relate to a consistent adult and set of peers on a day-to-day basis.

Even in multi-site settings, HighScope programs do not regularly rotate staff members between classrooms or centers. A rotational system is detrimental to the climate of trust that children depend on to venture forth into new relationships and learning. Having consistent people, like implementing a consistent daily routine, provides the stable base young children need to feel emotionally and physically secure. For this reason, HighScope settings, like all high-quality early childhood programs, also try to minimize staff turnover by creating a supportive work environment. Even if the program has student interns, or parent and community volunteers, these adults supplement but never replace the teaching team who support, teach, and care for the children every day.

Support the relationships that children establish with one another

Preschoolers who are forming relationships with one another might choose to work in the same area, share materials, talk with one another, sit together, engage in pretend play, or show concern for one another.

At work time in the book area, Pattie and Tanya read a book together in the beanbag chair.

❖

At outside time, Alex and Pater cover an area of the pavement with blue chalk. Alex says to Pater, "Let's pretend the blue is water!" Pater replies, "And there's snakes down there, and sea monsters." Alex adds, "So we have to stay up here on the step or they bite us!"

❖

At planning time, Josh asks Joseph to sit next to him at the table. Josh then makes a plan to play with Legos and says, "I want Joseph to play with me."

❖

At work time in the block area, Nona and Sally Mae sit in the cardboard box. Nona uses the flashlight to make "ghost tracks" on the walls of the box and tells a story about the "Ghost of Halloween." "Now it's your turn," she says, and gives the flashlight to Sally Mae.

❖

At work time at the sand table, when Tasha hurts her finger, Serena gives Tasha the red pail and shovel she is using. "Your shirt is red," she tells her. "This will make you feel better."

When daily observations show children forming friendships, teachers can use a number of strategies to support them. For example, you might put two children in the same planning and recall group so they can make plans to play together and jointly recall what they did. If the children's play revolves around certain ideas and materials, teachers can make sure these are plentiful and easy for the friends to access. Children might be encouraged to check out what their friends are doing at small-group time, sit together on a field trip, and interact in other ways.

At work time in the house area, Janie says to Elise, "Maybe I can ask my mom about you coming to my house." Elise replies, "I can see what is in your bedroom." Janie says, "I have a cat." When their mothers come to pick them up at the end of the day, their teacher mentions having overheard this conversation and the mothers arrange a play date.

Jamie and Eduardo play ball together every day at outside time. When their teacher reports this to Jamie's aunt and Eduardo's grandmother at a parent meeting, Jamie's aunt and Eduardo's grandmother make plans to take the two boys on the bus to the park over the coming weekend.

Provide opportunities for children to interact with others with whom they are less familiar

Friendships among preschoolers typically develop spontaneously, based on shared interests and compatible personalities. However, adults can create situations that allow children to interact with peers they might not ordinarily think to play with. For example, you might put two children who like to tell jokes in the same small group or ask the two children who were fascinated by the cider press to put the cider mill field trip pictures into an album together. Friendships can blossom as children discover mutual interests and skills; at the same time, new friendships give children rich exposure to classmates with backgrounds and personalities different from their own.

Adults can create situations in which children with similar interests can get to know one another.

By the same token, accept that it is also natural for young children to play alone or to play repeatedly with one or two friends. HighScope teachers do not require children to socialize, nor do they grow concerned when children engage in solitary or parallel play, or choose to play with the same friend(s) every day. Children should never be forced to "be friends" with others (DeVries & Zan, 1994). This negates their independent motivation and does not respect their emerging preferences. Children's relationships, just like those of adults, thrive when they are genuine and come from within. However, adults can intentionally create opportunities that allow children to discover interpersonal connections in unanticipated places and with unexpected people. Children, like adults, delight in the surprise of a new friend.

Refer children to one another

Another way you can support peer interactions is by referring children to one another, either for help solving a problem or as a source of ideas that children might choose to imitate and vary. Consider these two examples, both from small-group time.

Olivia is having trouble getting two pieces of clay to stick together and her teacher says, "I see Rudy attached his. Maybe he could show you how he did it." Rudy shows Olivia how he flattens the bottom of one piece and pushes it into the other. "Now you try," he tells her. After two attempts, Olivia succeeds. "Hello," she makes her clay figure say to Rudy's figure. "Hi," he makes his say back. They make their figures move closer together and giggle.

The teacher comments to the table of children, "I see Zach is bending his pipe cleaner into the letter Z for his name." Christina announces "I'm making a C for Christina." Muriel says, "I'm bending mine into a kitty." "Me too!" says Ben.

Such referrals among children serve multiple purposes. They promote social development by giving children concrete reasons to interact, thereby building trust and mutual respect. Another benefit is that encouraging children to turn to one another acknowledges their competence in solving problems and taking care of their own and others' needs. Children are then more likely to offer help on their own, and to turn to one another for assistance without adult prompting. (A side benefit is that teachers can continue to partner with children in play and not be constantly pulled away to solve problems throughout the classroom.)

At outside time, when Delilah approaches Katherine (a teacher) with a problem about getting a turn on the swing, Stella (another child) interjects, "I can help Delilah." Stella walks Delilah to the tire swing and talks to Ashley and Thomas about giving Delilah a turn.

❖

At work time, Malcolm tries to drag two long blocks, one in each hand, to the rug to build a launch for a "rocket boat race." The blocks bang into one another behind him and fall out of his hands. "This is too hard!" he says. "Robbie," he calls, "Come help me with these things!"

For examples of how preschoolers build relationships at different stages of development and how adults can scaffold their learning, see "Ideas for Scaffolding KDI 12. Building Relationships." These suggestions, together with strategies already described, will help children build relationships with you and others during play and other daily interactions.

Ideas for Scaffolding KDI 12. Building Relationships

Always support children at their current level and occasionally offer a gentle extension.

Earlier	Middle	Later

Children may

- Ask an adult for help or comfort.
- Play and work alone; occasionally watch and imitate peers.
- Exchange one or two words or gestures with others (e.g., pass a basket of spoons; answer a question with "yes" or "no").

Children may

- Ask an adult to play with them (e.g., "Will you do play dough with me?").
- Play and work alongside peers; occasionally interact (e.g., tell a peer what they are doing).
- Interact with others by alternating sentences or reciprocal actions (e.g., "My cat's name is Petunia. Do you have a cat?"; pass a basket of crayons back and forth as they draw alongside one another).

Children may

- Enjoy the company of an adult (e.g., seek out a particular teacher to cuddle or chat).
- Show preference for a special friend (e.g., plan to play together; call someone a friend; note when a friend is absent.)
- Sustain interactions; take conversational turns; share materials (e.g., "My dog chases balls." "Mine too. He slobbers on them." "Does yours chase squirrels?" "Yeah, and he barks").

To support children's current level, adults can

- Give help and comfort if asked; connect with individual children.
- Use children's names with one another; note if they imitate peers (e.g., "Leo, you're pounding golf tees in the clay like Gabe").
- Acknowledge when children interact with you and each other (e.g., "Lila, you passed the spoons to Mikki").

To support children's current level, adults can

- Warmly accept children's invitations to play with them.
- Offer materials that encourage interactions (e.g., blocks too long or heavy for one child to carry; riding toys that accommodate more than one child).
- Comment on children's interactions (e.g., "You and Nathan talked about cats").

To support children's current level, adults can

- Acknowledge children like playing with them (e.g., smile: "You seem to enjoy spending time with me").
- Create opportunities for friends to be together; encourage friendships to continue (e.g., put friends in the same small group).
- Listen and encourage children to listen to one another.

To offer a gentle extension, adults can

- Invite children to play and work alongside them (e.g., "I've got some blocks. Would you like to build with me?").
- Make connections to children with similar interests (e.g., "You like to paint and so does Olivia. Do you ever see her painting when you are at the easel?").
- To encourage exchanges, copy what children do, pause, and see if they reciprocate (e.g., stack blocks like the children, pause for a response).

To offer a gentle extension, adults can

- While playing with children, initiate conversations with them (e.g., while making play dough cookies, talk about the foods both child and adult like to eat).
- Label and describe friendships that they see among the children (e.g., "You and Carrie and Tony have been giggling together. It looks like you guys are friends").
- Interpret children's overtures to one another (e.g., "Nathan is handing you the pot. It looks like he wants to cook with you").

To offer a gentle extension, adults can

- Talk with children about what connects them (e.g., "We both giggle at the end of this book").
- Help children become aware of their developing friendships; comment that they enjoy being together (e.g., "Casey and Dylan, you always like to play together").
- Provide time and space (open and cozy) for children's interactions; respect choices about who they want to spend time with.

CHAPTER 9

KDI 13. Cooperative Play

B. Social and Emotional Development

13. Cooperative play: Children engage in cooperative play.

Description: Children involve adults and peers in their play. They engage in cooperative play with others by sharing materials, space, conversation, and ideas.

At work time in the block area, Christian makes a police officer bus by lining up chairs in rows and using the rolling pin as a steering wheel. He invites other children to ride the bus, and Timmy, Leila, and Theron sit down. Christian announces, "We're gonna catch speeders," and Leila says, "There's a fast one over there!"

At work time in the toy area, Gabrielle, Mariah, and Ellie play "dog school." Gabrielle says she is teaching the dogs how to do tricks. Mariah does a somersault and Ellie rolls over.

At snacktime, Zachary wants to get the attention of the child next to him, so he makes his teddy graham pretend to talk to the other child. "Yum, yum, I like honey," Zachary has his cookie say. "Me too," says the other child's bear. They pretend to lick honey off their bears' hands.

Cooperative play (also called collaborative play) means playing and working with others, and includes sharing toys, space, friends, attention, conversations, resources, skills, and ideas. When children play collaboratively, they work toward a common goal, such as building a block structure together or elaborating on a pretend play theme. Cooperation involves understanding the rights of others, interacting without being overly directive or submissive, differentiating intentional versus accidental actions, treating others as you would like to be treated, and balancing your own needs with those of others (Szaton, E. S., 1992). Preschoolers are beginning to develop these abilities and apply them to social interactions.

How Cooperative Play Develops

The foundations of cooperative or collaborative play appear in the sociability of infants. They generally orient toward peers at 2 months, make simple gestures by 3–4 months, and direct smiles and vocalizations by 6 months to get the attention of others. When babies begin to imitate one another at 9–12 months, it is the beginning of play, as though they are saying "I know what you're doing, so let's do it together!" (National Research Council & Institute of Medicine, 2000). Sequential actions with peers in the first year are followed by parallel play (often in the second year), and cooperative or reciprocal play (often in the third year).

During preschool, the length of these interactions and their reciprocity increases. In fact, researchers are beginning to rethink the importance of peer interactions in development as they discover that cooperative play is far more complex, sophisticated, and multifaceted than earlier believed (Vandell et al., 2006). For example, preschoolers' emerging capacities for perspective- and turn-taking lay the groundwork to coordinate play with others. Language development also facilitates cooperative play. Children who speak more clearly and communicate their ideas better have an easier time starting and keeping play going, says play researcher Carollee Howes (1988). Greater emotional self-regulation (KDI 9. Emotions) also helps children work through social problems and sustain episodes of collaborative interaction.

At work time in the block area, Kovid and Josh assume the roles of the plastic dinosaurs they are playing with. Kovid lifts one and says, "This dinosaur's name is Anthony." Josh addresses the dinosaur: "What do you want to do?" Kovid answers, "I want to fight." Josh says, "No way! We will have a talk about that." Kovid points to another dinosaur and says, "That one wants to kill us." Josh replies, "Let's get away." Kovid holds up a different dinosaur and tells Josh, "This is Robert." Josh says, "Is he nice?" and Kovid replies, "Yeah, but he's sleeping."

The number of children who can play together in a group also increases between the ages of three and five (National Research Council and Institute of Medicine, 2000). A younger child may play well with one other person, but the addition of a third is too difficult to manage. Over the next two years, as the ability to hold multiple images and people in mind increases, this same child can initiate and sustain complex play patterns with groups of peers.

All during work time, Peter and Jason play together, pretending to be sharks, building with Lego blocks, drawing sharks, and pretending to be scuba divers.

❖

At work time, Eli, Evan, Jason, Peter, and Isaac construct a marble runway together and send marbles down it.

❖

Matthew and Emily plan to "work at the office." They take phone calls, type on the keyboards, and put papers in envelopes. When other children and adults try to join their play, they say, "There are no more jobs here."

❖

At work time in the block area, Amanda "drives" Colin, Ashley, and Nicholas on the "bus" to the "church wedding." "Pick me up at 1:10," Colin tells her. Then she picks up her "dad," Isaac. After driving for a while, they go back to the church wedding, knock, and join the ceremony.

An increased capacity for cooperative play does not come "naturally" to children, however. While their desire for sociability may be strong, their interactions can be fragile. Distractions, frustrations, or misinterpreted cues can easily break up their play. For these reasons, adults are very important in structuring an environment that determines how much, how long, and how well children play together. Despite concerns that increased time in child care might slightly elevate young children's aggression, an important finding of the National Institute of Child Health and Human Development (NICHD) Early Childhood Care Research Network (Belsky, 2002; NICHD, 2006) is that higher quality child care is generally related to more competent peer

Teaching Strategies That Support Cooperative Play

General strategies that support social and emotional development (see chapter 2), such as arranging the room to accommodate sustained interactions and scheduling group times in the daily routine, can promote cooperative play. In addition, adults can use the specific strategies that follow to facilitate collaboration between children throughout the program day.

Encourage children to plan, work, and recall together

Encouraging children to make plans to work together acknowledges the importance of their collaboration and friendship. Work time provides many opportunities to follow up on their initial ideas and add jointly to the detail and complexity of their plans. Afterward, when children recall as a team, each one builds on the other's narrative and fills in additional pieces. Throughout the plan-do-review sequence, then, children experience the satisfaction of having their individual ideas respected and elaborated upon by one or more peers. In addition, when adults acknowledge these cooperative efforts ("I saw you each holding one end to carry the heavy blocks to the house area"), children are further encouraged to work together in the future.

At planning time, Kovid and Brianna say they are going to cook "pancakes" for the teacher. "We can flip them with the spatula," says Kovid. "Let's make hot chocolate too!" suggests Brianna, and Kovid agrees enthusiastically. "I'll stir it with the wooden spoon," adds Brianna.

❖

At work time in the block area, Evan and Quincy make a tent by putting a blanket over chairs. When Dottie asks to play, Evan says, "Sure, you can help put the blanket on."

At outside time, Anna and Jessa decide to roll some tires down the slide. Anna goes up the ladder first, holding the railing with one hand and the tire with the other. Jessa pushes the tire from behind and calls out encouragement. "We're getting it….It's almost up!" Once they get both tires in position at the top of the slide, they call to the children below. "Stay back so the tire won't hit you!" When the way is clear, they let the tires roll down the slide.

At recall time, Jeremy says he played Candy Land with Emily. "I landed on Gum Drop Mountain," he reports. "Me too," says Emily, "and we both picked purple cards."

Because children are carrying out their own intentions during these times of the day, rather than performing a structured activity designed by adults, they are free to explore a wide range of ideas and learn from one another. Collaborative play helps preschoolers consider other ideas and see things from multiple perspectives. Young children also challenge one another's thinking when they play cooperatively. Sometimes this happens through conflict or differences of opinion. A statement such as "Mine has more than yours!" can inspire them to devise a way of measuring to find out which child is right. Other times, they learn from differences in experience, such as when role-playing Thanksgiving dinner and one says to the other, "My grandma put water chestnuts in the stuffing. They were crunchy!"

Encouraging children to plan together fosters cooperative play.

Provide opportunities for collaboration at group times

When HighScope teaching teams plan small- and large-group times, they consider experiences that will explicitly encourage collaborative play. For example, they might give children balls and ask them to think of ways to pass them to one another. A group might meet outdoors so children can wash doll clothes or playground equipment. This invites preschoolers to collaborate as they carry water pails or divide the tasks of washing, wringing, hanging, or drying items. If the group-time involves building with Legos, teachers can offer children a choice of using a small (one-person) base or a larger (two-person)

base. Children who choose to work in pairs can then negotiate what they will build, where on the base it will go, its dimensions and colors, and so on.

At small-group time, Corey and Jeff invent a game with beanbags and hollow blocks. Corey says to Jeff, "First I throw all mine in and then you throw all yours in. Okay?" Jeff agrees and says he will count how many Corey gets in. They take turns throwing and counting.

At outside time, Tommy and Randy dig a big hole in the sandbox, fill it with water using the

garden hose, and sail the wooden boats they made earlier at the workbench. After seeing other interested children join them, the teacher plans a small-group activity for the following day to build things with sticks and twigs and various fastening devices. During the small-group time, children hold things for one another as they tie, tape, and glue the parts together.

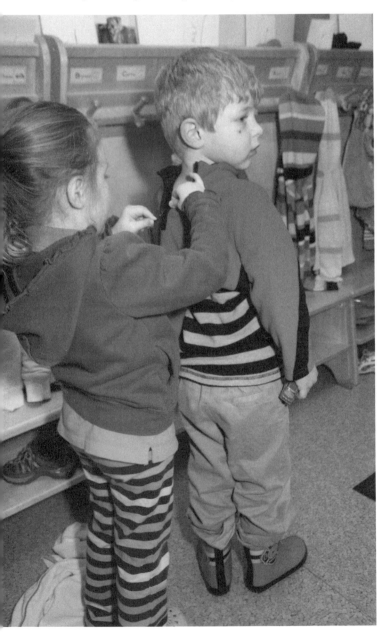

These children cooperate as one helps another with clothing before outside time.

Other ideas include children collaborating on an imaginary voyage, each contributing items to take onboard or suggesting the sights they see. In a group discussion, you can solicit their ideas for a rotation system to share classroom chores, such as passing out snacks. Finally, large-group movement and music activities provide many opportunities for children to take turns leading and following. For example, one child can choose a song from the songbook for everyone to sing, or suggest a movement for others to copy. Other children might then suggest ways to vary the words in the song, or alter the suggested movement on the next round. These group-time options allow children to share and expand on one another's ideas, which is the essence of cooperative play.

Help aggressive or withdrawn children join their peers

Some children need extra help before they can negotiate cooperative play on their own. They may push their way into the play setting too forcefully or hesitate to approach their peers at all. It is important to remember that such children are not (mis)behaving willfully or with negative intent. Like children engaged in social conflict, they have not yet learned how to become part of a group play situation. Teachers can help forceful or shy children learn the necessary skills in several ways.

For example, you can coach children who enter a group too aggressively. Observe with them from the sidelines, validate their desire to join the play, and offer or discuss their ideas on how to do this. Suggest noninvasive strategies by saying something like, "Maybe if you help carry blocks, they'll let you build the tower with them." Make comments or ask questions that help them consider the consequences of their ideas.

Forming Partnerships With Emerging Players

Chelsea, Callie, Corrin, Alana, Ben, Douglas, and Petey liked to play "moms," "dads," and "sisters" who went "dancing" and to the "movies," leaving the "baby" home with the "babysitter." Mikey tried to join this play, but his entry technique — growling and swiping at things — only made the others tell him to go away.

After observing Mikey's unsuccessful attempt to join the play, Beth, an adult, thought of a way she might help. The next morning, when the players were gathering and assigning roles, she asked if she could be the baby (one of the least desirable roles because everybody else could boss "the baby" around). On this day, even the sitter went to the movies, leaving "baby" Beth all by herself. Seeing Mikey lingering nearby, she said to him, "Mikey, would you like to be my doggy?" This suited Mikey because growling was a legitimate dog behavior. When the "family" and "babysitter" returned, the first thing they asked was "What's Mikey doing here?" Beth explained, "He's my doggy. He's very obedient, and he likes to eat dog food."

When the others had taken this information in and tested the "doggy's" ability to obey and to eat dog food, they accepted Mikey into their play. Seeing that Mikey was accepted into the role of doggy, Beth withdrew, leaving Mikey on his own with the group. Over time, Mikey graduated to the baby role, and several months later, when the role players turned to a new theme (barbershop play), Mikey was one of the first "customers" and even gave a few haircuts himself.

There are several things Beth did that enabled Mikey to be a successful member of the role-play group:

- Beth viewed Mikey's intentions in a positive manner. She assumed from the outset that Mikey wanted to join the play, even though his initial actions had a negative impact on the other children.

- Beth understood the structure of the ongoing play and asked for the least powerful role for herself. This gave her a legitimate inside position from which she could be a partner with Mikey without disrupting the play or displacing another player.

- Beth invited Mikey in during a natural break in the play. Rather than imposing her intentions on the other players at the height of their play, she chose a moment when they were occupied elsewhere, and she and Mikey could try out their partnership at their own pace.

- Beth took advantage of Mikey's ability to growl by offering him the role of a dog, thus giving him a chance to use his growling strategy in an appropriate context and to good effect.

- Beth withdrew from the play as soon as it looked as if Mikey could be partners with some of the other players on his own.

Although each child and each play situation is unique, this example illustrates the kinds of strategies adults can use to help young children join others in play.

At work time in the house area, Cassie says, "I could go for some Chinese!" She adds, "I'll be the orderer" and tells the other children where to sit at the table. Martha (a teacher) sees Alix approaching from the toy area. The previous day, Alix had been rebuffed by this group. Martha kneels beside Alix, acknowledges she wants to play restaurant too, and talks about how she might do that. "I want to be the orderer," says Alix. "Cassie's the orderer," Martha reminds her, "but maybe they need someone to be something else." "I could be the cook," suggests Alix. "That might work," says Martha. "Would you like to ask?" Alix approaches the group and Cassie agrees. "You can be the cook who fries the shrimp in the pan."

Sometimes you will observe children who want to become play partners but have not quite figured out how to do so. In such cases, it may be appropriate for adults to become partners with children, so children have the opportunity to develop the skills needed to participate with their peers. Adults can acknowledge children's play intentions and help them practice playing in the safe context of partnering with an adult. The adult can then help the child gain entry into the play scenario with peers, and gently withdraw once the child seems ready to handle the situation on his or her own.

At the other end of the social continuum are children who may be so fearful of rejection that they do not even attempt to enter into cooperative play. Regular group times, when children can play alongside peers without having to orchestrate it themselves, provide them with safe opportunities and may ease their anxiety over time. But sometimes withdrawn children benefit from a specific invitation that gives them an option (but never a requirement) to participate more actively. One strategy is to use a concrete (physical) aid that gives such

children the "power" to act as a group member. A device such as a "talking stick," for example, can embolden those who are shy or quiet. Consultant Emily Vance (2004, personal correspondence) offers the following example:

At greeting circle, the teacher invites children to tell the group about something they saw on the class walk. She gives the first child a "talking stick" and each child passes it to the next one who wants to speak. Those who do not want to speak are not pressured to do so. However, the teacher notices that even children who are often shy or reserved feel "empowered" when they hold the talking stick and take a turn speaking before passing it to a peer.

As already discussed (see KDI 8. Sense of competence), giving children the opportunity to act as leaders during large-group time can instill a sense of competence in young children. It can also promote peer collaboration. Even shy children rarely turn down a chance to offer an idea to the group when explicitly invited to do so. When they see peers accepting their suggestions, it may embolden them to risk entering into cooperative play at child-initiated times of the day. This risk-taking will happen gradually, as trust in their teachers, their peers, and above all, in themselves, is established and flourishes.

Play as partners with children

Teachers model cooperation when they act as partners in children's play. To join in children's activities, get down on their level, imitate their use of materials, and follow their ideas. Use the authentic conversational strategies described earlier (see KDI 12. Building relationships).

At work time in the house area, Gina and Lily declare their restaurant is open for business. Beth, their teacher, asks if she can order lunch.

Adults in HighScope programs work as partners with children, orienting themselves on the children's physical level and imitating what the children do.

"What do you want?" asks Gina. Beth says she's hungry and orders a sandwich, salad, and large glass of lemonade. "We only have soup and cupcakes at this restaurant," says Lily. "What kinds do you have?" asks Beth. "Tomato soup and chocolate cupcakes," answers Lily. "Then that's what I'll order," says Beth. "Coming right up" says Gina, and she puts a bowl, a plate, and eating utensils on the table.

When partnering with children, make sure you let them take the lead. Act out the roles and assume the attributes they assign you. For example, if a child says, "You're the dog and you chase me," then that is what you should do — even if you'd rather be a monster, or you're tired of being the chaser and you think it's the child's turn to catch you. You can try to extend the play by asking whether you should be a certain type of dog or make a particular chasing sound. If this idea appeals to the child, he or she will let you know. You might also try a small variation (growling or running toward the book area), but be sensitive to the response. The child may elaborate on the idea and take the lead in extending it. But if the child objects, or does not pick up on your innovation, drop it and continue playing according to the directions established by the child.

For examples of how children engage in cooperative play at different stages of development and how adults can scaffold learning at each level, see "Ideas for Scaffolding KDI 13. Cooperative Play" on page 96. Use the ideas on the chart, together with those described in the foregoing section, to support and gently extend children's cooperative play during your daily interactions with them.

Ideas for Scaffolding KDI 13. Cooperative Play

Always support children at their current level and occasionally offer a gentle extension.

Earlier	Middle	Later

Children may

- Carry out activities by themselves; engage in parallel play using similar materials.
- Have contact with another child in a play situation (e.g., one child pulls another in the wagon at outside time, one child holds a tube for another child at the water table).

Children may

- Begin to play in a similar way with another child (e.g., two children are playing with dinosaur figures; occasionally they talk together about what their figures are doing, and then they go back to their own play).
- Play with another child in simple play scenarios (e.g., play mommy and baby in the house area).

Children may

- Engage in collaborative play, that is, doing something together, taking ideas and contributions from each person (e.g., build a farm together with block structures and animals).
- Play with other children in complex play scenarios; invite other children to join their play and assign roles among themselves, give each other directions about what to do or how the situation should evolve.

To support children's current level, adults can

- Call attention to what other children are doing (e.g., "Vera is painting").
- Acknowledge when children are playing with other children (e.g., "You are pulling Suzie in the wagon. You are playing together").

To support children's current level, adults can

- Facilitate play between two children using the same materials (e.g., play with blocks simultaneously with two children, eventually incorporating both into the same play).
- Acknowledge play scenarios between children; call them by their role names (e.g., "Hi Mom! What seems to be making your baby cry?").

To support children's current level, adults can

- Look for opportunities to introduce other children into the collaborative play (e.g., "Kara, some children are playing monster under the climber. Do you want to come with me and play too?").
- Allow time for children's play scenarios to develop in complexity and detail over time (i.e., over days and even weeks).

To offer a gentle extension, adults can

- Draw children's attention to others who are doing similar things (e.g., "Alma is using the funnel too. She has the big one and you have the little one").
- Look for children who need play partners and refer children to one another (e.g., "Tania was looking for someone to chase her. Would you like to play?").

To offer a gentle extension, adults can

- Gradually withdraw from children's play when the children are able to continue on their own (e.g., once the block building is advanced, the adult quietly turns to work with another child in the block area).
- Join in children's play themes, taking a supporting role; add simple variations within the play theme, if necessary (e.g., "I'm the little sister. Mom, can I give the baby a bottle?").

To offer a gentle extension, adults can

- Help children clarify and explain their play ideas to one another (e.g., "Justin has a different idea about how to make the cars go fast down the ramp. Let's listen to his ideas").
- Add materials to support play extensions (e.g., add large pieces of fabric that children can use as capes if they are playing superheroes).

KDI 14. Moral Development

B. Social and Emotional Development
14. Moral development: Children develop an internal sense of right and wrong.

Description: Children develop ethical behavior. They understand that there are moral principles that do not vary by situation (e.g., people should not hit others).

At cleanup time, when Ezra puts all the caps back on the markers, Shona asks him if he drew a picture. Ezra shakes his head no and says he worked at the computer. Then he adds, "If I don't cover the markers, no one can draw a picture tomorrow. Whoever used them should have put the caps back on."

At snacktime, while passing around a bowl of fruit salad, Brianna tells her teacher, "Only one spoon until everyone gets some. Otherwise it isn't fair."

At work time in the house area, Ari is playing with two hand puppets. He makes one puppet "say" to the other, "No hitting ever, ever. It hurts!"

At work time at the computer station, Sylvester moves over to make room for another chair so Gabriella can join him and Chris. "You've been waiting a long time," he tells her, "and we've been playing forever!"

How Moralilty Develops

Morality is an internalized system of deciding whether behavior is right or wrong, apart from external punishment or sanctions. Our moral identity answers the question, "What kind of person do I want to be?" Moral development (also called having a conscience, superego, or ethical principles) is a long and complex process. It begins in toddlerhood, with concrete ideas such as it is wrong to hurt others, and extends well into adolescence and even adulthood as people form abstract moral values, such as the concept of equality and how it should govern our behavior.

Theories of moral development

Piaget (1932/1965) was among the first psychologists to study moral development in children. He observed how they made up rules for games and constructed ideas about behavior such as cheating and lying. In the early stages of moral reasoning, children focus on outcomes rather than intentions, and rigidly obey rules. As they interact with peers, they begin to consider behavior from other perspectives and apply

Piaget's Observations of Moral Development in Young Children

• •

The psychologist Jean Piaget (1932/1965) interviewed children about acts such as stealing and lying. When asked what a lie is, younger children (early preschool) answered that they were "naughty words." When asked why they should not lie, they again could not explain it beyond citing the forbidden nature of the act: "Because it is a naughty word." However, older children (later preschool) were able to explain, "Because it isn't right" or "It isn't true." That is, they cited simple moral reasons. Even older children (beginning primary grades) indicated intention as being relevant to the meaning and judgment of an act: "A lie is when you deceive someone else, but to make a mistake is just when you make a mistake."

— Epstein (2009, p. 101)

rules more selectively, based on mutual respect and reciprocity. In this way, social experiences lead to more advanced moral reasoning.

Piaget's work was elaborated on by Lawrence Kohlberg and his colleagues (Power, Higgins, & Kohlberg, 1989), who described a three-step developmental progression from self-interest to conformity with rules to a more socially oriented or principled system for judging behavior. Subsequent research, called "domain theory" (Turiel, 1983, 2002; Smetana, 2006), found that children's social interactions lead them to differentiate between "moral" behaviors that apply regardless of the situation and "conventional" rules that fluctuate. For example, four-year-olds say it is neither okay to wear pajamas to school (a convention) nor to hit another child for no reason (a moral principle). But when asked whether these actions would be okay if the teacher allowed them, most children say wearing pajamas would now be fine, but hitting still is not.

Based on these and other streams of theory and research, a complete and complex picture of early moral development is now taking shape. We now know it begins at a younger age than we thought. Evolutionary psychologist Steven Pinker (2008) confirms that "The stirrings of morality emerge early. Toddlers spontaneously offer toys and help to others and try to comfort people they see in distress" (p. 36). Between 18 and 22 months, children respond emotionally to what they view as a "violation of standards." Says psychologist Robert Emde (1998), the toddler not only wants to "get it right," but can become upset when an expectation about the way things "should be" is violated, for example, by a broken doll or a dirty toy. Children also begin to assess their own behavior in light of what is expected.

Moral issues important to preschoolers

Preschoolers wrestle with questions of moral behavior, particularly with regard to the treatment of others. Developmental psychologists Rheta DeVries and Betty Zan (1994) emphasize that moral development at this stage is still characterized by concrete thinking and observation of results. However, children gradually begin to consider the motivation behind the action and how it makes people feel, based on their own experiences.

At work time in the house area, Rachel says that a child is "cheating." When her teacher asks what she means, Rachel responds, "That means he's hurting someone's feelings."

Emerging cognitive abilities allow preschoolers to see the logical consequences of their actions. If they tear the pages from a book, no one in the class can read it. If they do not return materials where they belong, no one can find them the next day. Even if children do not at first see these connections on their own, they can if adults point them out. Seeing cause-effect relationships lets them begin to develop simple moral principles to govern their own and others' behavior.

Older preschoolers can also begin to grapple with the motivation behind an action. They want to know whether harmful behavior is "accidental" or "intentional." For example, they recognize that knocking over a block tower because you weren't paying attention when you ran past is not the same as knocking it over because you are mad at the builder. While children sometimes claim "It was an accident" as a way of denying responsibility or avoiding punishment (merely mimicking adults), they are also genuinely interested in determining whether hurtful behavior was or was not deliberate. The ability to differentiate intent is still fragile — preschoolers still focus primarily on the consequences of their actions — but it does emerge along with other classification skills. Moral development, differentiating "right" from "wrong," is a type of social classification.

At outside time, Casey runs into Maribelle while he's riding a bike. He gets off the bike and says, "I'm really sorry. It was an accident." Then he gives her a hug. "It's okay. You didn't hurt me," Maribelle reassures him. Casey looks relieved. "Do you want to ride the bike now?" he offers.

Teaching Strategies That Support Moral Development

To a great extent, young children learn morality from the examples they see at home and in the classroom. To help preschoolers develop a sense of morality, early childhood teachers can use the following support strategies.

Model moral behavior

Be consistent and fair-minded in all your interactions with children. They will learn the principles of kindness and equality when you establish and act upon clear expectations for their behavior, and also your own. Always emphasize problem solving rather than blame or punishment when children make social mistakes. When children offer solutions to social conflicts, make sure they are clear to everyone, doable, and that everyone agrees before putting them into effect. Avoid indefinite or abstract solutions. Children need to see a direct relationship between their behavior and its result. If the connection is unclear, the solution or outcome takes on a life of its own, and the cause-effect relationship is lost to the child.

Remember as well that moral education is not just encouraging children to treat others fairly or kindly. Moral principles also underlie *how* we engage young children in learning. Psychologist Cary Buzzelli (1996) says "conceptualizing teaching as inherently a moral activity means that we, as early childhood educators, must consider the moral implications of all the activities that occur in our classrooms" (p. 534). For example, teacher-child discourse is one way that teachers convey their own moral values and act as role models. In early childhood programs, how adults talk and act with young children determines whether children see themselves as self-initiating and competent learners who are treated with dignity and respect by adults, *or* they see themselves as the recipients of learning whose role is to absorb the lessons adults and authority figures transmit to them.

Instructional strategies influence the development of moral reasoning. An authoritarian, sit-still-and-listen approach to teaching and learning, for example, limits children's opportunities to engage in the give-and-take of problem solving and critical thinking that contribute to advanced moral development. By contrast, an active inquiry-based approach to teaching and learning encourages children to express ideas, try them out, and receive feedback from adults and peers in all domains of learning, including the development of moral principles.

State situations that involve moral matters in simple cause-and-effect terms

Lengthy or abstract statements of moral principles make no sense to young children. They need simple explanations in concrete terms. For example, you might say, "I'm making sure every child who wants birthday cake gets a piece before giving out seconds. It wouldn't be right if someone gets two pieces before every child

has one." Children will pick up on these simple statements and begin to use them on their own. You may hear these explanations stated not only in terms of their actions toward other people, but also applied to the treatment of animals and plants:

At snack time Madison says, "Next time I'm never ever going to take all the crackers because now there aren't too much left for everyone else."

At outside time, playing in the grass alongside the paved area of the playground, Casey finds a roly-poly. He moves it closer to the bushes, saying, "If we don't move it, somebody is going to step on it."

When adults describe situations that involve right and wrong in factual, nonjudgmental terms, children develop moral reasoning and an ability to see others' perspectives.

To deal with immediate classroom situations that involve right and wrong, describe the actions you see and their effects in factual, nonjudgmental terms. For example, you might say, "Karl, you walked over to Jamie's tower and pushed it with both hands, and now Jamie is crying. Jamie says he feels bad because he worked really hard on it and now all the pieces are on the floor. Karl, you say you are a strong robot who breaks things." Phrased in this way, the matter becomes open to problem solving by the children themselves (KDI 15. Conflict resolution), plus you are giving them the opportunity on their own with your support to wrestle with a child-sized moral issue: Is it okay or not okay for a robot to knock over a non-robot's tower? Working through such a problem and generating possible solutions will advance their growing capacity for understanding moral principles (in this case, the pros and cons of caring for others' work and feelings versus hurting others' work and feelings).

Acknowledge children's moral behaviors

Adults often think that if children feel good about themselves, they will do the right thing. But moral development does not arise from self-esteem. In fact, says developmental psychologist William Damon (1990), it is the opposite. Children who do the right thing feel good about themselves. By acknowledging (not praising) children's moral behavior, we help them become more aware of what they did and its positive effects on others. The child's internal social drive — the desire to have good relationships with others — becomes a motivating factor in acting morally.

At small-group time, while doing puzzles at the table, Jerzy says, "I want to help Christian with the panda [puzzle]." He moves next to Christian, but when Christian shakes his head to indicate he doesn't want help, Jerzy sits back down and

Taking turns in an early sign of moral development.

begins working on another puzzle. His teacher says, "You paid attention to Christian when he showed that he did not want help."

Involve parents to achieve as much consistency as possible between home and school values

Parents play a critical role in children's moral development. Damon (1990) says a consistent and stable parental influence helps children act morally, even when peers or other outside forces pull them in different directions. Teachers can support parents as they deal with today's challenges, such as media messages, that may contradict their own value system.

Teachers and parents do well to appreciate the family's vital role as a child's first and most important model of moral behavior. What parents do and say leaves a large and lasting impression. Parents also provide or can learn to provide moral instruction to young children. For example, parents can help children understand the effects of their behavior on the emotions of their siblings and playmates. Researcher Nancy Eisenberg (1989) found that rather than a parent saying, "Don't hit your sister," moral development was more positively affected by comments such as, "When you hit your sister, it made her sad." Teachers can support this strategy by sharing with parents classroom examples of how they have attempted to convey such simple and concrete cause-effect messages to children in noncritical and nonpunishing ways.

Remember that you are not in competition with parents for a child's moral identity. Not only is it inappropriate for a teacher to take on this role, it is disrespectful to the parent and confusing for the child. There will be times, however, when home and classroom beliefs diverge. Speak openly and honestly with parents when this occurs. Accept rather than judge differences (except in cases of abuse and neglect), and problem-solve any potential conflicts in how situations are handled in the two locations.

Often differences reflect variations in social conventions, while the underlying moral principle is the same. For example, parents and teachers may hold different views about eating. They share a moral value that grown-ups are responsible for feeding children healthy food. However, the healthy food served at home (such as cooked carrots) is eaten with utensils, while the healthy food served at school (such as cheese cubes) can be eaten with one's fingers. Clarifying both the commonality and the differences in this case can help you reach a mutually acceptable resolution.

For examples of how young children show their emerging sense of morality at different stages of development and how adults can scaffold learning at each level, see "Ideas for Scaffolding KDI 14. Moral Development" on page 104. The chart provides ideas for carrying out the foregoing strategies as you play and interact with children throughout the program day.

Ideas for Scaffolding KDI 14. Moral Development

Always support children at their current level and occasionally offer a gentle extension.

Earlier	Middle	Later
Children may	*Children may*	*Children may*
• Be unaware of how their behavior affects others (e.g., continue playing with blocks after another child complains, "Hey! You knocked over our control tower!").	• See how their behavior affects others when an adult points it out (e.g., When the teacher says, "Beth cried when you hit her," Donna responds, "I made her sad").	• Realize on their own how their behavior affects others; may try to make amends (e.g., say genuinely, "Oops, I bumped it" and help another child restack the blocks).
• Be unaware that some behavior is acceptable and some is unacceptable (e.g., take toys from others).	• Be aware what behavior is acceptable but still act on self-interest (e.g., "It's not fair he took all the crackers, so I'm taking all the cheese").	• Increasingly act according to their understanding of acceptable and unacceptable behavior (e.g., "You're not supposed to take toys. Give it back to me.")
• Be unaware of moral principles (e.g., laughs when their juice spills on another child's crackers).	• Be unable to differentiate intentional from accidental behavior (e.g., "He's bad. He spilled juice on my crackers").	• Differentiate purposeful from accidental behavior (e.g., "My crackers got wet, but you didn't mean to spill juice on them").
To support children's current level, adults can	*To support children's current level, adults can*	*To support children's current level, adults can*
• Point out when children's behavior affects others (e.g., "You knocked over Ben's block tower").	• Note when children acknowledge the effects of their behavior after an adult points it out ("Yes, that made Beth sad").	• Comment when children spontaneously acknowledge how their behavior affects others (e.g., "You helped rebuild Sasha's tower after you accidentally bumped it").
• State expectations for acceptable and unacceptable behavior (e.g., "Please listen while Jamie tells us her idea for how to move").	• Acknowledge children's awareness of acceptable and unacceptable behavior (e.g., "Taking all the crackers isn't fair").	• Affirm when children act morally (e.g., "You asked Fiona to give the toy back").
• Stop hurtful or upsetting behavior.	• Reframe statements to focus on behavior rather than people (e.g., when a child labels another child "bad," say, "Hitting is bad").	• Note when children differentiate accidental from purposeful behavior (e.g., "You saw that what happened was an accident").
To offer a gentle extension, adults can	*To offer a gentle extension, adults can*	*To offer a gentle extension, adults can*
• Describe how children's behavior affects others (e.g., "When you took her truck, Sara got angry").	• Without judging, encourage children to see the effects of their behavior (e.g., "What did Paige do after you took the book?").	• Ask how children can make amends (if they do not do so on their own) (e.g., "How could you help Sasha rebuild her tower?").
• Point out children's acceptable behavior (e.g., "You're listening to Jamie's idea").	• Encourage children to act on moral principles (e.g., "Taking all the cheese isn't fair either. What else could you do?").	• Articulate the principles behind children's moral behavior (e.g., "You asked Fiona for the toy because we shouldn't hurt others").
• Point out the connection between children's behavior and moral principles (e.g., "Hitting hurts"; "You're done with the computer. Now it's Jesse's turn").	• Label when behaviors are accidental rather than purposeful (e.g., "Oops. He bumped into you. I think it was an accident").	• Discuss intentional vs. accidental behavior (e.g., ripping a page when you're mad vs. being excited to see what happens next).

CHAPTER 11

KDI 15. Conflict Resolution

B. Social and Emotional Development
15. Conflict resolution: Children resolve social conflicts.

Description: Children engage in conflict resolution, or social problem solving, to settle interpersonal differences. They identify the problem, offer and listen to others' ideas, and choose a solution that is agreeable to all.

At work time, when Andre bumps into the cups Justin is stacking, Justin stands up, stomps his feet, clenches his fists, and yells, "Hey, that's my tower." Later, when Andre sits in the computer chair before Justin can, Justin says, "Hey, you're not my friend. Leave me alone."

At work time in the block area, Monty comes over to his teacher and says, "He keeps stepping on my toys. Can you tell him to stop?"

At work time in the house area, Zeke and Mariah want the same pan lid. Their teacher asks for their ideas on how to solve the problem. Zeke says he can make a lid. He gets a piece of paper, traces around the pot, and cuts it out with scissors.

At outside time, Makenna gets off the bicycle to look at a turtle. Becky asks her, "Could I ride your bike while you look at the turtle? I'll give it back in a little while."

Conflict resolution is the use of appropriate nonaggressive strategies to settle interpersonal differences. Other terms for this behavior include *social problem solving* and *conflict mediation*. To emphasize that children are not misbehaving, but rather making mistakes as they learn to deal with social conflicts, it is best to avoid negative or judgmental terms such as anger management, behavior management, or classroom discipline. As early childhood educator and HighScope field consultant Betsy Evans says, "Children don't misbehave, they make mistakes" (2002, p. 13). Psychologist Daniel Gartrell (1995) adds that when we see children's actions as mistakes rather than "bad behaviors," we can respond with kindness and understanding instead of punishment.

When young children get into conflicts with others, they do not aim to be mean or hurtful. They are simply goal-oriented. For example, they may want to play with a toy or sit next to the teacher while she reads a story. Their actions are focused on getting what they want without regard for the effect of their behavior on others. Children may also be imitating aggressive behavior they see elsewhere (at home or in the media) without having learned that violence or verbal abuse are not socially acceptable ways of dealing with social problems in the classroom, or elsewhere.

Resolving conflicts when needs and emotions run high is a complex process and involves a great deal of learning. Given that adults are not always effective at social problem solving, it

Children's Social Conflicts Are Mistakes, Not Bad Behavior

• •

As I look back now on my years working with young children, I see that a change eventually occurred in my own attitude about their conflicts, and that this change came about as a direct result of my efforts to understand and use a problem-solving approach during these episodes. As I explored and learned how to apply the strategies of conflict mediation with young children, I discovered not only that dealing with conflict could be a satisfying and enjoyable part of teaching but also that children, when given support, were enormously capable problem solvers. The moments I had once dreaded as a teacher and a parent gradually became opportunities for the children to learn new skills and for me to deepen and enrich my perceptions of children. Conflicts became occasions for hope; the children and I were learning together that diverse points of view need not lead to unresolved frustration and anger. Instead we were discovering that conflicts and disputes can actually be a starting point for honest exchanges that lead to stronger and more gratifying relationships.

— Evans (2002, pp. 3–4)

is no wonder that this area poses a substantial challenge for young children. It is also a major concern among practitioners, many of whom have not been trained to deal with this daily occurrence.

How Conflict Resolution Develops

The capacity to resolve conflicts is highly dependent on children's emotional and social abilities in other domains. Because conflicts elicit strong feelings, children must be able to recognize, label, and regulate their emotions (KDI 9. Emotions). Finding solutions involves seeing another's perspective, and draws upon the emerging capacity for empathy (KDI 10. Empathy). The desire and means to negotiate and act on a mutually determined resolution further draws on a broad set of social behaviors including creating community (KDI 11. Community), working cooperatively (KDI 13. Cooperative play), and being guided by moral principles (KDI 14. Moral development). Thus the mastery of conflict resolution skills is not only a separate strand of development, but also reflects the trajectory of growth described in these other areas. For example:

- *Recognizing and labeling emotions* — At the same time they are learning to resolve conflicts, preschoolers are learning to identify and regulate their emotions. Although this can be difficult, they are developing two abilities that can assist them. First, language helps children label and describe their feelings. Just attaching words to emotions can help them calm down. Second, preschoolers can defer gratification, at least for short periods of time, because they can imagine (again, mentally picture) how and when their desires will be fulfilled.

- *Feeling empathy* — Understanding another person's viewpoint requires the mental capacity to imagine thoughts, feelings, and actions outside oneself. This ability begins in infancy and continues to emerge in preschool. Because young children can project their own experiences onto others, they are capable of modifying their behavior to bring about a different result.

- *Developing a sense of community* — The motivation to be part of the community helps preschoolers balance their own wishes against those of other group members. Preschoolers meld these individual and group concerns as they make the transition from "me" to "we." Engaging in conflict resolution allows them to meet both their personal and affiliative needs.

- *Engaging in cooperative play* — Preschoolers can collaborate with others to reach a common goal. Such interactions involve paying attention to playmates, regulating one's own behavior, and imagining what you and others might say and do in a play scenario. Similarly, dealing with conflict requires one to picture "what if" in order to arrive at a solution.

- *Developing a framework for moral behavior* — Young children's growing appreciation for moral principles and social conventions can help them resolve conflicts. They are concerned with the treatment of others ("hitting is wrong"), and have rudimentary ideas

about fairness ("no seconds until everyone gets firsts"). They are also familiar with certain social norms ("a timer is an accepted way to keep track of turns; impatience is not"). Preschoolers can use their knowledge of these moral principles and social conventions to resolve conflicts.

Teaching Strategies That Support Conflict Resolution

Adults are often uncomfortable with children's social conflicts and eager to get them over with. Researcher Sandra Lamm and her colleagues (Lamm, Groulx, Hansen, Patton, & Slaton, 2006) identified three common teacher responses to children's disagreements: *pleading* (begging children to take turns or "be nice and share"),

Adults help children learn to resolve conflicts by listening to their feelings and helping them acknowledge others' point of view.

directing (telling children not to take toys from others or to "use your words"), or *punishing* (assigning children time-outs or withdrawing privileges). These strategies may impose short-term solutions — sometimes no more than momentary ones — but they do not bring about long-term changes or build children's social problem-solving competencies.

It is more helpful when teachers see children's social mistakes as learning opportunities. Rather than intervening, adults can guide the problem-solving process with appropriate modeling and support. This requires patience and practice, but research shows that preschool children can master the steps in conflict resolution. Moreover, when they do, there is a 40 percent decrease in challenging behaviors such as crying, tattling, and physical aggression (Lamm et al., 2006).

The following are strategies teachers can use to prevent social conflicts and turn them into learning experiences when they inevitably arise. Adults who use these techniques often report that their own ability to solve interpersonal problems at home and with coworkers also improves. When you and your children learn and practice the steps of conflict resolution, disagreements can cease to be a source of threat and become an opportunity for learning and building bridges of peace and respect.

Establish a safe classroom with clear expectations

A teacher's first job is to create a positive and safe environment in the classroom. Psychologist Diane Levin (2003) says children need to know the following four things are safe: their bodies; their feelings; their thoughts, ideas, and words; and their work. Reassure children you will not allow them to be physically or verbally hurt, and that you will immediately stop any harmful or dangerous behavior, including aggression, name calling, and rejection. Your words and deeds should also let children know they will never be physically punished, shamed, or deprived of basic needs.

Model strategies for self-calming. In addition to overall safety, children need to know strategies for calming themselves down so they can feel "safe" with their emotions. Use the strategies that you know work with particular children. These might include pouring water or sand at the texture table, hugging a teddy bear, or working with play dough or other sensory materials. In addition, provide a quiet place where children can calm down, furnished with soft materials such as rugs, pillows, and beanbag chairs.

Promote consistency in the environment. A program environment for preventing and dealing with social conflicts depends on the general teaching strategies described in chapter 2. These include a consistent daily routine, which eliminates the "surprises" that can cause anxiety and in turn provoke children to act angrily or disruptively. A well-organized and labeled room gives children choices and a sense of control over their environment, which in turn promotes emotional self-control. Open traffic patterns and lack of crowding and clutter keep them from bumping into one another and knocking over someone's else's work. Too much openness, however, such as having all the furniture pushed up against the wall, can encourage running and accidents.

Making their own choices and decisions has resulted in fewer behavior problems in the classroom. Because children are actively learning, there is no time for boredom. There is less crying, fighting, hitting, kicking, and "s/he has mine." (A HighScope Teacher)

Provide plentiful materials. Ample and diverse materials are also important in preventing social conflicts. Match materials to children's emerging developmental abilities. Inappropriate toys may lead to frustration or boredom. Where possible, provide multiple sets of materials, especially popular ones, to avoid conflicts over scarce resources. Give children tools, such as various types of timers, that will help them find workable solutions to using equipment and materials that must be shared.

At work time in the toy area, David and Joseph want the same airplane. The teacher holds the airplane while she and the children talk about the problem. David says, "I wanted it first." Joseph says, "No, it's mine!" The teacher says, "You both want to use the airplane," and looks to the boys for confirmation. They both nod. "What can we do to solve this problem?" the teacher asks. David says, "We can take turns." Joseph says, "Me first. I'll get the timer." David says, "He can have it. Then it will be my turn." The teacher says, "So, it sounds to me like you are both agreeing that Joseph will use the airplane first and that you will use the timer to show when a turn is up." Again, both boys nod in agreement. The teacher hands the plane to Joseph. David turns the sand time over to start Joseph's turn.

Plan well for few transitions. Because change is difficult for young children, challenging behaviors frequently occur during transition times. Therefore, minimize the number of transitions, keep them short, and plan for their occurrence. Helpful strategies include the following:

- Give warnings shortly before an activity ends. Encourage children to help you, for example, by flicking the lights or starting the cleanup music.

- Minimize waiting time. Prepare materials beforehand and start an activity as soon as children begin to arrive.

- Allow adequate time for transitions so children do not feel rushed or pressured. For example, provide enough time for young learners to put on their jackets before outside time.

- Provide reasonable choices to keep children engaged, such as moving in different ways from large-group time to the snack table. When children are given choices about when and how they transition, they are more involved in the next activity (Hemmeter & Ostrosky, 2003).

- Be flexible. Whenever possible, let children finish what they are doing before transitioning to the next activity. For example, a child can finish a small-group project before joining the others at the large-group rug.

For additional strategies on handling transitions, see *"I Know What's Next!" Preschool Transitions Without Tears or Turmoil* by Betsy Evans (2007).

Set consistent limits. Finally, provide clear and consistent limits for children. Just as having a predictable schedule and space helps them feel in control, so does knowing what behaviors are and are not acceptable. Use simple and concrete language when explaining your expectations. For example, say "Hitting hurts" rather than "I cannot allow violence in the classroom." Once expectations are set, be consistent about implementing them. Share them with parents, and solicit their input, so they can work with you in explaining and supporting classroom expectations with their children. Parents sometimes comment that it is easier for them to set expectations at home (concerning interactions between siblings, for example) when they can model their behavior after the consistency shown by teachers in the classroom. Having the same expectations at home and school is also reassuring for children.

Providing plentiful materials helps prevent confilcts over scarce resources.

Use a multistep approach to conflict resolution

Social conflicts are inevitable in an early childhood setting. Many times it is unclear how a conflict started or why the children are upset. The solution is not always obvious either.

At outside time, Alice and Sam are dressing up in the playhouse. At the same moment, they reach for a colorful scarf. They tug it back and forth, yelling, "I got it first! Give it to me!"

At the snack table, Grace wants to sit close to Tilda. Tilda begins to gently push her away. Grace says, "I want to sit there." Ellen (a teacher) acknowledges that Grace wants to stay where she is and asks Grace and Tilda what they can do to solve the problem of them being too close. Grace says she can move her chair, and then moves it a bit further away.*

At work time at the sand table, Ashley and Christian want the same funnel. Sue (a teacher) asks for ideas to solve the problem. Lili, standing nearby, says, "Ashley can have mine when I'm done, and Christian can keep the other one." Sue asks Ashley if that's okay. When Ashley hesitates, but is unable to say why she is still concerned, Sue asks her, "You look concerned. Do you want to know when Lili will be done?" Ashley nods and

Lili says, "I'll get the sand timer and turn it over once. Then you can have it." Sue turns to Ashley, who nods her okay.

❖

Jacob and Sam disagree over the new necklaces in the house area. When the teacher asks how they can solve the problem, Jacob says, "We need more new necklaces." Since this is not possible, the teacher is about to ask the boys for another idea. To her surprise, however, Sam says, "Yeah!" and goes to the art area to get leather thongs and beads. The boys spend the rest of work time making necklaces and wristbands with hidden "spy phones" inside.

To help children resolve social conflicts when they do occur, HighScope teachers receive training in a six-step problem solving approach to conflict resolution (detailed in Evans, 2002). Here each step is described with an example. When teachers use these six steps and feel confident about their ability to handle social conflicts, they not only help young children learn important social lessons, they also encourage language development, reflection, and problem solving in general. (For a summary with additional examples, see "Steps in Resolving Conflicts With Preschoolers" on pp. 116–117. Also see "Adopting a Problem-Solving Approach to Conflict" in chapter 2 of *The HighScope Preschool Curriculum* [Epstein & Hohmann, 2012].)

Step 1. Approach calmly, stopping any hurtful actions. Children should always feel safe and secure, perhaps especially in the midst of a conflict. When you remain calm, it helps children regain control. Therefore, place yourself between the children, get down on their level, use a calm voice and gentle touch, and do not take sides. If an object (such as a toy)

is involved in the dispute, hold it yourself. This "neutralizes" the object so children can become engaged during the rest of the problem-solving steps.

Emma and Joe are building a dinosaur house together. When Joe accidentally knocks part of it down, Emma pushes him, saying, "Get out!" Their teacher, observing this interaction, comes over and places herself between the children and the house they are building. She kneels down between the children and gently puts an arm around each of them.

Step 2. Acknowledge children's feelings. Emotions often run high during a conflict because children feel strongly about their desires. Helping children express their feelings — and accepting their feelings without judgment — allows children to let go of their emotions. Only then can children begin to identify and solve the problem. Use simple words to help children label their feelings, for example, "You look really upset." You may need to acknowledge feelings several times before you are ready to move on to the next step.

The adult acknowledges, "Emma, you sound angry with Joe. And Joe, you look sad. I can see that part of the dinosaur house has fallen down."

Step 3. Gather information. It is important for all the children involved to express their point of view. You and other adults need the information, the children need to have their say, and everyone can benefit from listening to the others state what they need in the situation. You might start by asking an open-ended question such as, "What's the problem?"

The adult asks each child, "What's the problem? Can you tell me what happened?"

Step 4. Restate the problem. Restating the problem — "So the problem is…" — without taking sides or jumping in with your own solution lets children know you are truly listening. Repeat the children's words, or rephrase them if the words are hurtful or unclear. For example, if a child says, "He's a dummy. He took my block," you might say, "You're upset because Vic took the block off the top of your tower." Check with the children to make sure you have stated the problem correctly, and allow them to add more information, if necessary.

The adult says, "Joe, you don't want Emma to push you, and Emma, you don't want Joe to build because he is knocking the house down. Is that right?" They nod their heads.

Step 5. Ask for ideas for solutions and choose one together. You might begin by asking, "What can we do to solve this problem?" Encourage children to propose a solution, and give them ample time to think and respond. Accept all the ideas children offer, even if some do not seem realistic. If the children draw a blank, you might offer an idea or two to get them started. Help children think through the consequences of implementing their ideas and encourage *them* to pick one. Sometimes, an idea that adults think is unworkable or unfair may end up working just fine for the children. Once the children choose a solution, make sure that each child is comfortable with it.

Adult: You both still want to build the dinosaur house. What can we do to solve the problem?

Emma: I want to build this part by myself. Joe can build over there.

Joe: I want to build something for the dinosaurs too.

Adult: It sounds like Joe wants to build something for the dinosaurs too. What else do you think the dinosaurs need? What do you have at your house?

Joe: I have a swimming pool at my house. I could build that.

Adult: That's an idea.

Joe: Hey, I can build the dinosaurs a swimming pool just like mine!

Emma: Yeah!

Adult: So, Emma is going to keep building the dinosaur house here *(points to the stack of blocks)* and Joe is going to build a dinosaur swimming pool in this space *(points to the area next to the dinosaur house). (Emma and Joe nod their heads yes and turn back to the blocks. Emma rebuilds the dinosaur house while Joe starts building the swimming pool.)*

Step 6. Give follow-up support as needed. Acknowledge that the *children* have solved the problem. ("You solved the problem!") As children return to their play, stay nearby to make sure the solution is working and everyone is satisfied. You may help carry out the solution. If a problem remains, repeat the process with the children to find another approach.

The adult says, "Emma and Joe, you solved the problem! You both talked about ideas for solving your problem together. And you listened to each other carefully. I'd like to see the dinosaur house and swimming pool when they are finished."

Remember that children need time and many repetitions to understand and use the steps in conflict resolution. Adult support is crucial as they master this process. If you are patient, however, you may find that children begin to use the steps on their own.

At work time in the block area, Michala and Christopher argue over who will play with the toy animals. "We have a problem," Christopher says. "How can we solve it?" Michala replies, "I know! You can have these, and I can have these."

Supportive adults in HighScope programs help children learn to master the conflict resolution process.

Christopher accepts this solution. "Hey," he yells across the room to their teacher. "We solved the problem!"

At lunch, Russ and Tony argue over who can sit in the chair next to Charles. Charles says to them, "Don't fight. There's lots more choices." The boys move one of the other chairs at the table closer to Charles, on his other side. All three children eat and talk together at lunch.

Help children reflect on problem-solving strategies apart from actual conflict situations

Sometimes it is easier for children to learn overarching lessons after a conflict has passed, when emotions are not running so high. You can review the episode and acknowledge their success in resolving it later, for example, during snacktime or as you dig alongside them at outside time.

You can also deal more generally with the topic of conflict resolution by reading books, sharing songs, and telling stories about people coping with similar social conflicts. Children will often spontaneously talk about their own comparable experiences. You can also encourage discussion with comments ("That reminds me of when we almost missed the bus yesterday") and open-ended questions ("Johnny was mad in the story when his baby brother broke his racing car. Did something like that ever happen to you?").

Children also explore conflict resolution when they role play scenarios with puppets, dolls, or other props. In fact, all the creative arts provide nonthreatening ways for children to express the feelings that are aroused in social conflicts and represent various solutions. Another useful technique is called a "social story." The adult introduces a common problem — for example, at greeting circle — and the children share their ideas about how to solve it.

One day a group of children is playing with toys in the block area. They leave to go to the art area, and another group of children begins playing with the toys in the block area. The first group comes back and says, "Those are our toys. You can't play with them." The children worked out a solution, but this has been a common enough problem that the teachers decided to do a "social story" about it.

The next day, at greeting circle, the teachers post several large sheets of paper that tell the story of the previous day's events with stick figures and captions. They title the story "When Children Leave" and pose the question "What can we do to solve this problem?" The children offer various solutions that the teachers write down: They could share (divide) the toys; they could all play together; the second group should give the toys back; the first group has to wait their turn. The class assembles the pages into a book, which is added to the book area. Whenever a similar problem arises, the children look at the book and either use one of their solutions or add another one (Epstein, 2009, p. 121).

Other typical problems that can be addressed with social stories include children sharing time on toys or equipment for which there is a limited supply (one computer or rocking boat), or children spilling water in the block area as they carry it to the house area. Social stories can also be used to help individual children deal with interpersonal situations or problems, such as entering into play without taking away toys or telling the others what to do. You can make up a personal story book about the problem that the child can refer to whenever this situation comes up. (For an illustrated example of this type of personal social story, see "Using Social Stories to Help Resolve Common Conflicts" on pp. 118–119.)

For examples of how young children resolve social conflicts at different stages of development and how adults can support and gently extend their learning in this KDI, see "Ideas for Scaffolding KDI 15. Conflict Resolution" on page 120. Use these ideas (in addition to those already detailed) in your daily play and other interactions with the children in your preschool program.

Steps in Resolving Conflicts With Preschoolers

1. Approach calmly, stopping any hurtful actions.

- Place yourself between the children, on their level.
- Let children know you need to hold any object in question.
- Use a calm voice and gentle touch.
- Remain neutral rather than take sides.

At work time in the house area, Ella and Kevin both reach for the large wooden spoon at the same time. Ella slaps Kevin's hand and yells, "I want it." Kevin makes a fist. José, their teacher, comes over and kneels down. He gently takes the keys from Ella and says, "Let me hold these while we solve this problem." He puts one arm around Kevin and strokes his hand. Kevin leans into him and relaxes his fist. José puts his other arm around Ella. José says, "We can't hit because it hurts. But we can talk. Tell me what happened." He listens calmly as the children each express their intentions to stir the "bear soup" with the spoon.[2]

2. Acknowledge children's feelings.

- "You look really upset."

Sydney and Olivia tug in opposite directions on the beanbag chair. When their teacher, Amy, comes over, Sydney says she wants to sit in the chair and read a book to her baby doll. Olivia says that Sydney, who is younger, "is too little and dumb to read" and that she wants the chair to look at a book herself. Sydney yells, "No!" Amy says, "It sounds like you are both upset because you each want to sit in the chair." The girls nod. Amy sits on the floor a slight distance away from the chair. Sydney sits down a few inches from her, while Olivia sits right next to Amy and puts her head on her shoulder. Acknowledging that each child seeks comfort in a different way, Amy smiles directly at Sydney and puts her arm around Olivia. She turns to Olivia and says, "Sydney is upset because she wants to read to her doll." She turns to Sydney and says, "Olivia is upset because she wants to read in the chair, too. Let's see how we can solve this problem." After problem solving, the girls agree they can sit in the chair together and take turns reading to the doll.

3. Gather information.

- "What's the problem?"

Marcus stands alongside the "tunnel" he's built with Jamal, gripping a red car in his clenched fist. Jamal kneels on the floor, his back turned to Marcus, shooting the blue and yellow cars through the tunnel. "Is there a problem?" their teacher, Lucy, asks. "He's making them go too fast. They'll crash," answers Marcus. "It's a race," says Jamal. Franklin, standing nearby, says, "Marcus took the red car. Jamal had it first." Lucy looks at Marcus, who says, "Because he was gonna crash it."

Lucy asks the boys if she can hold the cars and then summarizes, "It sounds like Marcus wants the cars to race fast and Jamal wants them to go slow." "Not slow," corrects Jamal, "just not crash." Lucy amends, "So it's okay if they go fast, but not so fast that they crash?" Jamal nods yes. "I can make 'em go fast but they don't crash," says Franklin. "Is it okay if Franklin shows us how he does that?" asks Lucy. Marcus and Jamal agree and Lucy hands Franklin the cars. The three boys race cars "Franklin's way" until it is time to clean up.

---

[2]Anecdotes from Epstein (2009, pp. 116–119).

4. Restate the problem.

- "So the problem is…"

Devon points at Matthew and says, "He's stupid!" Their teacher says, "You are angry at him because he kicked over your tower." Devon says, "I'm really mad. I worked on it all morning!"

5. Ask for ideas for solutions and choose one together.

- "What can we do to solve this problem?"

- Encourage *children* to think of a solution.

At work time in the block area, Ben and Mariah want to sit in the same chair on the "pizza truck." Their teacher asks what they can do to solve the problem. Christian, standing nearby, says, "They could have two chairs." The teacher asks if that is okay and Ben and Mariah agree. Together Ben and Mariah bring over a second chair, which Ben sits in, and then Mariah takes the first chair.

6. Give follow-up support as needed.

- "You solved the problem!"

- Stay near the children.

- Repeat the process if necessary.

Lane and Brian agree it will be Lane's turn at the computer after Brian has used it for two flips of the sand timer. As the end of the second flip nears, their teacher looks toward the computer area to make sure the changeover happens as agreed. Brian says, "Here, Lane," and switches chairs to watch and offer his ideas. Lane and Brian continue to take turns at the computer and talk for the next 15 minutes.

Using Social Stories to Help Resolve Common Conflicts

Talking about common conflicts in moments of calm — when they are not happening — can make it easier for children to think about the problem and offer solutions. "Social stories" are an effective way to bring up typical classroom problems and discuss children's ideas for solving them. Adults can turn them into "storybooks" that children can refer to when these conflicts occur again. Here is an example of a social story in which a child talks about joining others safely in play.

1

I Want to Play!

2

3

4

Sometimes children are playing and I want to play too.

5

I want them to see me and to know that I want to play.

6

7 I could ask a teacher to help me play with children.

Can you help me — I want to play.

8 Sometimes I get really excited. Things break and children get hurt.

9 It is okay to get excited, but when I hurt children and toys, children get upset

10 I will keep things and children safe. I will not throw, hit, or break things.

11 It's fun to play with children when we are all safe.

12 the end

(Reprinted from *Me, You, Us: Social-Emotional Learning in Preschool,* by Ann S. Epstein, PhD, 2009, HighScope Press, pp. 122–123)

Ideas for Scaffolding KDI 15. Conflict Resolution

Always support children at their current level and occasionally offer a gentle extension.

Earlier	Middle	Later

Children may

- Be unaware that there is a conflict; respond to a conflict with yelling or physical action.
- Be unable to suggest a solution.
- Walk away from the problem-solving process.

Children may

- Identify the problem in a conflict situation (e.g., "She took my truck").
- Suggest a solution; focus on their own solution (e.g., "I have an idea. I go first").
- Solve conflicts with adult assistance.

Children may

- State the problem and give a description of what happened in a conflict situation (e.g., "I was playing with the truck and she took it. I want it back").
- Suggest solutions; consider the solutions proposed by others.
- Solve conflicts on their own without adult mediation (e.g., say to another child, "We have a problem. How can we solve it?", then share solutions, choose one, and carry it out).

To support children's current level, adults can

- Describe what you observe and stop hurtful behavior.
- Ask children if you can offer a solution if they can't; suggest one and get their responses.
- Accept when children walk away from the problem-solving process.

To support children's current level, adults can

- Listen to each child identify the problem, remaining neutral (not taking sides).
- Restate child's solution (e.g., "So your idea is that you go first").
- Acknowledge when children solve a problem with your assistance (e.g., "You solved the problem. You're going to build together").

To support children's current level, adults can

- Add details to the children's description of the problem ("So you need a doll to feed, and you need a doll to give a bath to").
- Restate all the proposed solutions (e.g., "So Sue's idea is that you build together, and Max's idea is that he builds first and then Sue takes a turn").
- Acknowledge when children solve a problem on their own (e.g., "You didn't need my help. You solved the problem on your own!").

To offer a gentle extension, adults can

- Label the situation as a problem.
- Encourage children to think of a solution.
- Continue to attempt to engage children in the problem-solving process.

To offer a gentle extension, adults can

- Reframe the problem in a neutral way (e.g., "You both want to use the same truck").
- Encourage children to listen to the solutions proposed by others (e.g., "Let's listen to Katya's idea").
- If you observe that no one is being harmed, give children time to solve a problem on their own before stepping in to provide assistance.

To offer a gentle extension, adults can

- Encourage children to think about the details of the problem (e.g., "Is it that you want to use *this* truck, or do you need something to carry your blocks?").
- Affirm that there is more than one solution to a problem.
- Refer children to one another for help in resolving conflicts.

Social and Emotional Development Strategies: A Summary

General teaching strategies that support social and emotional development
- Create a supportive environment.
- Help children make the transition from home to school.
- Arrange and equip the classroom for social interactions.
- Implement predictable schedules and routines to create a secure community.
- Foster specific skills through modeling, coaching, and providing opportunities for practice.

Teaching strategies that support self-identity
- Focus on children throughout the day.
- Address diversity and differences positively.
- Provide nonstereotyped materials, activities, and role models.
- Encourage family members to become involved in the program.
- Establish ties with the community.

Teaching strategies that support a sense of competence
- Encourage self-help skills consistent with children's abilities and developmental levels.
- Scaffold learning by introducing the next level of challenge when children are ready to move on.
- Support children's ideas and initiatives.
- Acknowledge children's efforts and accomplishments.
- Provide opportunities for children to be leaders.

Teaching strategies that support emotions
- Accept children's full range of emotions as normal.
- Name or label children's emotions as well as your own.
- Call attention to the feelings of others.
- Comment on and discuss feelings throughout the day.

Teaching strategies that support empathy
- Model caring behavior.
- Acknowledge and label the feelings that children have in common.
- Create opportunities for children to act with empathy.
- Practice perspective-taking in nonsocial situations.

Teaching strategies that support community
- Create an atmosphere that fosters mutual respect and responsibility.
- Call attention to activities the whole class participates in.
- Involve children in the community outside the classroom.

Teaching strategies that support building relationships
- Interact with children in a genuine and authentic manner.
- Maintain a stable group of children and adults.
- Support the relationships that children establish with one another.
- Provide opportunities for children to interact with others with whom they are less familiar.
- Refer children to one another.

Teaching strategies that support cooperative play
- Encourage children to plan, work, and recall together.
- Provide opportunities for collaboration at group times.
- Help aggressive or withdrawn children join their peers.
- Play as partners with children.

Teaching strategies that support moral development
- Model moral behavior.
- State situations that involve moral matters in simple cause-and-effect terms.
- Acknowledge children's moral behaviors.
- Involve parents to achieve as much consistency as possible between home and school values.

Teaching strategies that support conflict resolution
- Establish a safe classroom with clear expectations.
- Use a multistep approach to conflict resolution.
- Help children reflect on problem-solving strategies apart from actual conflict situations.

References

American Academy of Pediatrics. (2006). *The importance of play in promoting healthy child development and maintaining strong parent-child bonds. Clinical report.* Elk Grove Village, IL: Author. doi:10.1542/peds.2006-2697

American Sign Language Browser. (2000). Michigan State University. Online at http://commtechlab.msu.edu/sites/aslweb/browser.htm

Atance, C. M., Bélanger, M., & Meltzoff, A. (2010). Preschoolers' understanding of others' desires: Fulfilling mine enhances my understanding of yours. *Developmental Psychology, 46*(6), 1505–1513.

Bandura, A. (1994). Self-efficacy. In V. S. Ramachaudran (Ed.), *Encyclopedia of human behavior* (Vol. 4, pp. 71–81). New York, NY: Academic Press.

Battistich, V., Solomon, D., & Watson, M. (1998, April). *Sense of community as a mediating factor in promoting children's social and ethical development.* Paper presented at the meeting of the American Educational Research Association, San Diego, CA.

Baumeister, R. F., Campbell, J. D., Krueger, J. L., & Vohs, K. D. (2004). Exploding the self-esteem myth. *Scientific American, 292*(1), 84–91. doi:10.1038/scientificamerican0105-84

Belsky, J. (2002). Quality counts: Amount of child care and children's social-emotional development. *Journal of Developmental and Behavioral Pediatrics, 23*, 167–170.

Bigler, R. S. (1997). Conceptual and methodological issues in the measurement of children's sex-typing. *Psychology of Women Quarterly, 21*, 53–69.

Buzzelli, C. A. (1996). The moral implications of teacher-child discourse in early childhood classrooms. *Early Childhood Research Quarterly, 11*, 515–534. doi:10.1016/S0885-2006(96)90020-4

Chess, S., & Alexander, T. (1996). Temperament. In M. Lewis (Ed.), *Child and adolescent psychiatry: A comprehensive textbook* (2nd ed., pp. 170–181). Baltimore, MD: Williams & Wilkins.

Clark, K. B., & Clark, M. P. (1947). Racial identification and preference in Negro children. In T. M. Newcomb & E. L. Hartley (Eds.), *Readings in social psychology* (pp. 169–178). New York, NY: Holt, Rinehart, & Winston.

Clements, D. H. (1999). The effective use of computers with young children. In J. V. Copley (Ed.), *Mathematics in the early years* (pp. 119–128). Reston, VA: National Council of Teachers of Mathematics and National Association for the Education of Young Children.

Cummings, C. (2000). *Winning strategies for classroom management.* Alexandria, VA: Association for Supervision and Curriculum Development.

Damon, W. (1990). *The moral child: Nurturing children's natural moral growth.* New York, NY: Free Press.

Daniels, M. (2001). *Dancing with words: Signing for hearing children's literacy.* Westport, CT: Bergin & Garvey.

Denham, S. (2006). The emotional basis of learning and development in early childhood education. In B. Spodek & O. N. Saracho (Eds.), *Handbook of research on the education of young children* (pp. 85–104). Mahwah, NJ: Erlbaum.

DeVries, R. & Zan, B. (1994). *Moral classrooms, moral children: Creating a constructivist atmosphere in early education.* New York, NY: Teachers College Press.

Diamond, K. E., & Innes, F. K. (2001). The origins of young children's attitudes toward peers with disabilities. In M. J. Guralnik (Ed.), *Early childhood inclusion: Focus on change* (pp. 159–178). Baltimore, MD: Brookes.

Dunn, J. (1998). *The beginnings of social understanding.* Cambridge, MA: Harvard University Press.

Eisenberg, N. (1989). The development of prosocial values. In N. Eisenberg, J. Reykowski, & E. Staub (Eds.). *Social and moral values: Individual and social perspectives* (pp. 87–102). Hillsdale, NJ: Erlbaum.

Eisenberg, N., Spinrad, T. L., & Sadovsky, A. (2006). Empathy-related responding in children. In M. Killen & J. G. Smetana (Eds.), *Handbook of moral development* (pp. 517–553). Mahwah, NJ: Lawrence Erlbaum.

Elias, M. J., Zins, J. E., Weissberg, K. S., Frey, M. T., Greenberg, N. M., Kessler, R.,… Shriver, T. P. (1997). *Promoting social and emotional learning: Guidelines for educators.* Alexandria, VA: Association for Supervision and Curriculum Development.

Emde, R. (1998). Early emotional development: New modes of thinking for research and intervention. *Pediatrics, 102*(5), 1236–1243.

Epstein, A. S. (1993). *Training for quality: Improving early childhood programs through systematic inservice training.* Ypsilanti, MI: HighScope Press.

Epstein, A. S. (2009). *Me, you, us: Social-emotional learning in preschool.* Ypsilanti, MI: HighScope Press.

Epstein, A. S., & Hohmann, M. (2012). *The HighScope Preschool Curriculum.* Ypsilanti, MI: HighScope Press.

Evans, B. (2002). *You can't come to my birthday party! Conflict resolution with young children.* Ypsilanti, MI: HighScope Press.

Evans, B. (2007). *"I know what's next!" Preschool transitions without tears or turmoil.* Ypsilanti, MI: HighScope Press.

Fox, L., & Lentini, R. H. (2006). "You got it!" Teaching social and emotional skills. *Young Children, 61*(6), 36–42.

Gartrell, D. (1995). Misbehavior or mistaken behavior? *Young Children, 50*(5), 27–34.

Giles, J. W., & Heymann, G. D. (2005a). Preschoolers use trait-relevant information to evaluate the appropriateness of an aggressive response. *Aggressive Behavior, 31*(5), 498–509. doi:10.1002/ab.20086

Giles, J. W., & Heymann, G. D. (2005b). Young children's beliefs about the relationship between gender and aggressive behavior. *Child Development, 76*(1), 107–121.

Handler, D. (2001). Storytelling with dolls: A powerful way of communicating with children. In N. A. Brickman (Ed.), *Supporting young learners* (Vol. 3, pp. 31–38). Ypsilanti, MI: HighScope Press.*

Hartup, W. W. (1986). On relationships and development. In W. W. Hartup & Z. Rubin (Eds.), *Relationships and development* (pp. 1–26). Hillsdale, NJ: Erlbaum.

Hartup, W. W., & Moore, S. G. (1990). Early peer relations: Developmental significance and prognostic implications. *Early Childhood Research Quarterly, 5*(1), 1–17. doi:10.1016/0885-2006(90)90002-I

Hemmeter, M. L., & Ostrosky, M. (2003). Classroom preventive practices. *Research synthesis on effective intervention procedures: Executive summary* (chapter 4).Tampa, FL: University of South Florida, Center for Evidence-Based Practice: Young Children with Challenging Behavior.

Hirschfield, I. A., & Gelman, S. A. (1997). What young children think about the relationship between language variation and social difference. *Cognitive Development, 12*, 213–238. doi:10.1016/S0885-2014(97)90014-9

Howes, C. (1987). Social competency with peers: Contribution from child care. *Early Childhood Research Quarterly, 2*(2), 155–167. doi:10.1016/0885-2006(87)90041-X

Howes, C. (1988). Peer interactions of young children. *Monographs of the Society for Research in Child Development, 53*(1, Serial No. 217). doi:10.2307/1166062

Hyson, M. (2004). *The emotional development of young children: Building an emotion-centered curriculum* (2nd ed.). Washington, DC: National Association for the Education of Young Children.

Jantz, R. K., & Seefeldt, C. (1999). Early childhood social studies. In C. Seefeldt (Ed.), *The early childhood curriculum: Current findings in theory and practice* (3rd ed., pp. 159–178). New York, NY: Teachers College Press.

Kagan, S. L., Moore, E., & Bredekamp, S. (Eds.). (1995, June). *Reconsidering children's early development and learning: Toward common views and vocabulary.* Goal 1 Technical Planning Group Report 95-03. Washington, DC: National Education Goals Panel.

Katz, L. (1993). *Dispositions, definitions, and implications for early childhood practice.* Champaign, IL: ERIC Clearing House on Elementary and Early Childhood Education.

Katz, L., & McClellan, D. (1997). *Fostering children's social competence: The teacher's role.* Washington, DC: National Association for the Education of Young Children.

Kohn, A. (1993/1999). *Punished by rewards: The trouble with gold stars, incentive plans, A's, praise, and other bribes.* Boston, MA: Houghton Mifflin.

Ladd, G. W., Birch, S. H., & Buhs, E. S. (1999). Children's social and scholastic lives in kindergarten: Related spheres of influence? *Child Development, 70*(6), 1373–1400.

Ladd, G. W., Herald, S. L., & Andrews, R. K. (2006). Young children's peer relations and social competence. In B. Spodek & O. N. Saracho (Eds.), *Handbook of research on the education of young children* (2nd ed., pp. 23–54). Mahwah, NJ: Lawrence Erlbaum.

*Also available at the HighScope *Extensions* archive at highscope.org.

Lamm, S., Groulx, J. G., Hansen, C., Patton, M. M., & Slaton, A. J. (2006). Creating environments for peaceful problem solving. *Young Children, 61*(6), 22–28.

Levin, D. E. (2003). *Teaching young children in violent times: Building a peaceable classroom* (2nd ed.). Washington, DC: Educators for Social Responsibility and National Association for the Education of Young Children.

Marsh, H., Ellis, L., & Craven, R. (2002). How do preschool children feel about themselves? Unraveling measurement and multidimensional self-concept structure. *Developmental Psychology, 38*(3), 376–393. doi:10.1037/0012-1649.38.3.376

Marvin, R. S., Greenberg, M. T., & Mossler, D. G. (1976). The early development of conceptual perspective taking: Distinguishing among multiple perspectives. *Child Development, 47*(2), 511–514. doi:10.2307/1128810

McCoy, C. L., & Masters, J. C. (1985). The development of children's strategies for the social control of emotion. *Child Development, 56*(5), 1214–1222.

Meece, J. L. (1997). *Child and adolescent development for educators.* New York, NY: McGraw-Hill.

Meltzoff, N. (1994). Relationship, the fourth 'R': The development of a classroom community. *School Community Journal, 4*(2), 13–26.

National Institute of Child Health and Human Development (NICHD). (2006, January). *The NICHD study of early care and youth development: Findings for children up to age 4½ years.* Washington, DC: US Department of Health and Human Services, National Institutes of Health, NICHD, NIH Pub. No. 05-4318.

National Institute for Early Education Research (NIEER). (2007a). Rx for behavior problems in pre-K. *Preschool Matters, 5*(5), 4–5.

National Institute for Early Education Research (NIEER). (2007b). Tools that address social development. *Preschool Matters, 5*(5), 2.

National Research Council. (2001). *Eager to learn: Educating our preschoolers.* Washington, DC: National Academies Press.

National Research Council and Institute of Medicine. (2000). *From neurons to neighborhoods: The science of early childhood development.* Washington, DC: National Academies Press.

Orellana, M. F. (1994). Appropriating the voice of the superheroes: Three preschoolers' bilingual language uses in play. *Early Childhood Research Quarterly, 9,* 171–193.

Perry, B. D. (1994). Neurobiological sequelae of childhood trauma: PTSD in children. In M. M. Murburg (Ed.), *Catecholamine function in post-traumatic stress disorder: Emerging concepts* (pp. 253–276). Washington, DC: American Psychiatric Press

Piaget, J. (1932/1965). *The moral judgment of the child.* New York, NY: Free Press.

Piaget, J. (1950). *The psychology of intelligence.* London, England: Routledge.

Pinker, S. (2008, January 13). The moral instinct. *The New York Times Magazine,* 32–37, 55–56, 59.

Pomerantz, E. M., Ruble, D. N., Frey, K. S., & Greulich. F. (1995). Meeting goals and confronting conflict: Children's changing perceptions of social comparison. *Child Development, 66*(3), 723–738.

Post, J., Hohmann, M., & Epstein, A. S. (2011). *Tender Care and early learning: Supporting infants and toddlers in child care settings* (2nd ed.). Ypsilanti, MI: HighScope Press.

Power, F. C., Higgins, A., & Kohlberg, L. (1989). *Lawrence Kohlberg's approach to moral education.* New York, NY: Columbia University Press.

Ramsey, P. G. (1991). The salience of race in young children's growing up in all-White community. *Journal of Educational Psychology, 83,* 28–34.

Randolph, J., & Gee, P. Center for Edication, Rice University School Literacy and Culture Project. (n.d.). *Building community in the classroom.* Retrieved November 8, 2007, from http://centerforeducation.rice.edu/SLC/Randolph011406.pdf

Raver, C. C., Garner, P. W., & Smith-Donald, R. (2007). The roles of emotion regulation and emotion knowledge for children's academic readiness. In R. C. Pianta, M. J. Cox, & K. L. Snow. (Eds.), *School readiness and the transition to kindergarten in the era of accountability* (pp. 121–147). Baltimore, MD: Brookes.

Rothbart, M. K., & Bates, J. E. (1998). Temperament. In W. Damon (Series Ed.) & N. Eisenberg (Volume Ed.), *Handbook of child psychology: Social, emotional, and personality development* (5th ed., Vol. 3, pp. 105–176). New York, NY: Wiley.

Rubin, K. H., Bukowski, W., & Parker, J. G. (2006). Peer interactions, relationships, and groups. In N. Eisenberg (Ed.), *Handbook of child psychology: Social, emotional, and personality development* (Vol. 3, pp. 571–645). New York, NY: Wiley.

Saarni, C. (1999). *The development of emotional competence.* New York, NY: Guilford.

Sendak, M. (1963). *Where the wild things are.* New York, NY: Harper & Row.

Smetana, J. G. (2006). Social domain theory: Consistencies and variations in children's moral and social judgments. In M. Killen & J. G. Smetana (Eds.), *Handbook of Moral Development* (pp. 119–154). Mahwah, NJ: Lawrence Erlbaum.

Sroufe, L. A., & Fleeson, J. (1986). Attachment and the construction of relationships. In W. W. Hartup & Z. Rubin (Eds.), *Relationships and development* (pp. 51–71). Hillsdale, NJ: Erlbaum.

Sylva, K. (1992). Conversations in the nursery: How they contribute to aspirations and plans. *Language and Education, 6*(2), 141–148. doi:10.1080/09500789209541333

Szanton, E. S. (1992). *Heart Start: The emotional foundations of school readiness.* Arlington, VA: Zero to Three/National Center for Clinical Infant Programs. Retrieved from ERIC database. (ED 352171)

Teglasi, H., & Epstein, S. (1998). Temperament and personality theory: The perspective of cognitive-experiential self-theory. *School Psychology Review, 27,* 534–550.

Thompson, R. (2009). Doing what doesn't come naturally: The development of self-regulation. *Zero to Three, 30*(2), 33–39.

Turiel, E. (1983). *The development of social knowledge: Morality and convention.* New York, NY: Cambridge University Press.

Vandell, D. L., Nenide, L., & Van Winkle, S. J. (2006). Peer relationships in early childhood. In K. McCartney & D. Phillips (Eds.), *Blackwell handbook of early childhood development* (pp. 455–470). Oxford, England: Blackwell.

Wellman, H. (2002). Understanding the psychological world: Developing a theory of mind. In U. Goswami (Ed.), *Handbook of childhood cognitive development* (pp. 167–187). Oxford, England: Blackwell.

Wood, D., McMahon, L., & Cranstoun, Y. (1980). *Working with under fives.* Ypsilanti, MI: HighScope Press.

Zahn-Waxler, C., Radke-Yarrow, M., Wagner, E., & Chapman, M. (1992). Development of concern for others. *Developmental Psychology, 28*(1), 126–136. doi:10.1037/0012-1649.28.1.126

Zeiger, J. (2007, February 25). Developing a community of learners. Retrieved from http://classroom-management-tips.suite101.com/article.cfm/developing_a_community_of_learners

About the Author

Ann S. Epstein, PhD, is the former Senior Director of Curriculum Development at HighScope, where she worked for 40 years. Her areas of expertise include curriculum development, professional development, research and program evaluation, and instrument development. Dr. Epstein's publications include *The Intentional Teacher; Essentials of Active Learning in Preschool; The HighScope Preschool Curriculum; Me, You, Us: Social-Emotional Learning in Preschool; Numbers Plus Preschool Mathematics Curriculum; Tender Care and Early Learning: Supporting Infants and Toddlers in Child Care Settings; Supporting Young Artists;* and *Small-Group Times to Scaffold Early Learning.* She was also a key developer of COR Advantage, an observational assessment of children from infancy through kindergarten, and the Program Quality Assessment for measuring teaching practices and program management. In addition to a PhD in Developmental Psychology, Dr. Epstein has a Master's of Fine Arts degree. She has shown her pieces in art exhibits and has published works of fiction.